GOD

HEALED

YOU

By Marybeth Wuenschel

Contributions
Crystal Hexamer, Jamie McCarthy, Pam Criss, Mark
Wuenschel, Kate Johnston, Sheila Lovelace

TABLE OF CONTENTS

IT'S HARD TO BELIEVE

This healing book is my attempt to bring to life the Word of God regarding healing. Jesus healed so many that if we were to get rid of all the healing and every demonic deliverance found in the Gospels, there would be very little left. God wants you well, healthy and whole and that is why Jesus healed over and over again. He couldn't help it. It is who he is. It is his nature to heal, and it is the Father's nature to heal. Jesus did nothing on his own. Everything Jesus did he did according to the will of the Father. It's the Father's will to heal. Jesus was ushering in a new kingdom, a whole new rule, the Kingdom of God.

Jesus healed then, and he hasn't changed. Jesus' healing power has not diminished. Jesus died but rose again. Jesus is alive, and He rules His Kingdom. The Bible says that He is the same yesterday, today and tomorrow (Hebrews 13:8) God made a decision to heal you, and he hasn't changed his mind. He still wants to heal you and deliver you from every evil and cleanse you of every sin. Let him. Jesus already died to heal you. He already took away your sins and sicknesses so you may as well accept it. Believe He did it just for you.

That evening many demon-possessed people were brought to Jesus. He cast out the evil spirits with a simple command, and he healed all the sick. ¹⁷This fulfilled the word of the Lord through the prophet Isaiah, who said, "He took our sicknesses and removed our diseases."
Matthew 8:16-17

I know, I know, it's hard to believe

It's hard to believe God can be that good, that he isn't holding anything against us or trying to teach us a lesson. It's hard to believe there isn't something we have to do to earn his love and healing. The only thing he wants to teach us is our need for him. He made us to be one with him. Without him, we are at the mercy of the merciless world. But with him all is ours. Hard to believe, I know, but that is just what God wants us to do; believe. He wants us to love him, follow him, serve him and trust him with our health, and welfare. He is our daddy, our provider, our protector, our defender, and our ever present help in time of need.

God is a covenant God and he declared us delivered, healed and free and sealed it with the blood of Jesus who laid down his life for us. God made a covenant with us and sealed it forever and ever with the blood of Jesus. It lasts throughout eternity, and God will not go back on his word. He made a decision to forgive us and heal us by sending his son to live and die for us.

He did it all for us, not so we can remain miserable, but so we can enjoy life and truly live (John 10:10).

Jesus came to deliver us from evil, save us from our sins, heal us and bring us life through the power of the Holy Spirit and by the will of God the Father, both here on earth and forever in heaven.

He went around all of Galilee, teaching in their synagogues, proclaiming the gospel of the kingdom, and curing every disease and illness among the people. His fame spread to all of Syria, and they brought to him all who were sick with various diseases and racked with pain, those who were possessed, lunatics, and paralytics, and he cured them. **Matthew 4:23-24**

GO THE DISTANCE IN PRAYER

MATTHEW 15:22-23 *And behold, a Canaanite woman of that district came and called out, "Have pity on me, Lord, Son of David! My daughter is tormented by a demon." But he did not say a word in answer to her. His disciples came and asked him, "Send her away, for she keeps calling out after us.*

The Canaanite woman, this scripture verse is referring to, heard the disciples tune her out and ask Jesus to get rid of her. Jesus himself said no to her TWICE, and she still kept asking. She would not give up. The Canaanite woman did not take no for an answer. She knew Jesus was her hope, her only hope, and her last resort. He was the answer for her daughter, she knew it and wasn't about to quit now. She knew who he was and was not afraid to approach him. She did not let the rebuke and disdain of Jesus' followers deter her.

Don't give up when you hear a bad report. So many times we pray for people and bad news follows and we get discouraged and give up believing that God wants to heal. Don't let a bad report or continued pain keep you from believing your healing is coming. It may be just around the corner.

Why do we give up too soon? I decided once not to let anything keep me from praying till the end. I picture myself as a lifeguard swimming out to sea to save a child from drowning. Would I stop swimming just because I am tired or it may be inconvenient? I may get tired on the way and want to quit, but there is a life at stake. I may have better things to do, but there is a life at stake. I think of it this way, what would the drowning child want from me. Would he or she want me to give up and say, "Well it might be God's will for that child to die today" or is it my duty to do whatever I can? It is my duty to go the distance.

BE BOLD go the distance. Be willing to fight. If you are fighting or struggling to believe God, hang on a little longer. Trust a little longer. Put out into the deep. Be willing to risk looking foolish. God can't resist you when you do.

STAND YOUR GROUND

Exodus 14:13-14

13 But Moses answered the people, "Do not fear! Stand your ground and see the victory the Lord will win for you today. For these Egyptians whom you see today you will never see again. 14 The Lord will fight for you; you have only to keep still."

HOW LONG have you been sick? How long have you been standing in faith waiting for your rescue? Are you sure you are standing in faith? Have you stood in faith or in fear? Have you stood in anticipation or in resignation? Have you stood your ground in the good times and in the bad? Have you stood your ground in the face of bad news, extreme reports or a depressing diagnosis? Have you stood your ground all the way to victory? If not, you have not stood long enough. There is always victory for you. Always. God only brings us through to victory. That is all he has in mind for you. Just believe, and rest assured.

What does it mean to stand your ground? How do I stand? What do I do? You stand by resting, waiting, trusting and believing God wants only good things for you and is fighting on your behalf.

Jeremiah 29:11 *For I know well the plans I have in mind for you, says the Lord, plans for your welfare and not for woe, plans to give you a future full of hope.*

Don't give in to fear or other negative thoughts. The word of God is a weapon, and it is to be used. The Israelites had just left Egypt. God rescued them from slavery. As soon as Pharaoh, the King of Egypt let the people go, he changed his mind and had the army pursue them right up to the Red Sea. The people were panicking with the sea in front of them and the army closing in behind them. God promised the Israelites they would never see the Egyptians again all they had to do was follow. Moses lead the people into the Red Sea, and they followed. God is saying the same thing to you and me and all of God's children. Do not fear, stand your ground, don't quit now, don't quit believing in the miracle. I am about to open up the sea.

Read Jeremiah 29:11 and believe it to be true for you and speak it out. When you say what God says about you, faith rises up in you. Say this.... "God has great plans for me. He is on my side and has a good future in store for me!" If you are complaining or depressed and afraid for your future, than it's time to change your words. Your thoughts and feelings will follow your words. Speak words of fear, and you will remain fearful, speak words of faith,, and you will be faithful.

Start speaking words of life. This will help you to rise above any situation and cling to hope. You always have a choice between hope and despair. Remind yourself daily that you have more faith in God than in your present circumstances. This will help you stand your ground and hold on to faith and keep fear at bay.

Trust that God is fighting for you. Don't trust in what you see or feel in the natural or physical realm. Trust in the supernatural. Just like the Israelites saw God work wonders that day, you too will see whatever you are willing to believe in. God is fighting your battle for you. Rest in that knowledge and stand your ground. HOLD THE FORT. When you trust in God, you are standing on solid ground. Don't give any ground to fear. Don't let those thoughts of fear or death or worry take hold of you and rob you of your hope and peace and trust. Say HA!!!!! I am trusting in God. He has me and will not let anything happen to me. You can say this with confidence because you are hanging on to his word which is as good as his promise.

PSALM 91:9-10, *"Because you have made the Lord, who is my refuge, Even the Most High, your dwelling place,*[10] *No evil shall befall you, nor shall any plague come near your dwelling;"*

JUST SAY THE WORD

Matthew 8: 8-9 *The centurion said in reply, "Lord, I am not worthy to have you enter under my roof; only say the word and my servant will be healed. ⁹ For I too am a person subject to authority, with soldiers subject to me. And I say to one, 'Go,' and he goes; and to another, 'Come here,' and he comes; and to my slave, 'Do this,' and he does it."*

Do you have anyone obeying you? I am not an officer and have no first-hand knowledge of this kind of obedience. My kids were raised to obey, but I can honestly say I don't know what's it like to hear " Yes Ma'am, right away Ma'am." This officer in the Roman Army had a hundred men obeying his every command. He understood authority, and he recognized Jesus' authority. This centurion believed in Jesus and believed he was God. He knew he had supernatural power and commanded a supernatural army. The Centurion recognized the King of Kings.

This pagan soldier knew more about Jesus than the anyone of the people of Israel. Where did he get this knowledge? How did he come to know Jesus' power and might? He knew that Jesus only needed to say the word and the wind, the waves, the mountain, disease, sickness, even the stars, the sun, and the moon would obey without thinking twice. The Centurion believed that Jesus controlled the universe and everything in it with His word. This soldier recognized Jesus' authority and power and that he was God. "Only say the Word," the Centurion asked, and Jesus said, "it will be done for you just as you believed it would be done." This man was a believer, his faith was extraordinary, and Jesus blessed him for it.

In the Old Testament Gentiles were not allowed to share the same roof with a Jew, let alone a Rabbi. Gentiles knew their place among the Jews. The centurion knew where he ranked in relationship to Jesus. He knew he was not worthy to have Jesus come into his house. He knew where he stood and he still believed not only that Jesus could heal but that he would heal, even him a gentile. His faith was so complete; Jesus described it as "GREAT

FAITH."

The Centurion must have known not only the power and might of Jesus but also his heart. Jesus wants us to know that he loves us enough to heal us. Don't doubt it, be like the Centurion and expect his love for you his child. The Centurion believed in Jesus' love for him.

Faith is important to God. Believe he cares for you. Believe enough to ask with expectancy. Ask God and then believe he will do it for you. Often, though, something like this happens. Someone will ask for prayer because they are desperate and right after prayer they continue to complain as if they hadn't prayed at all.

Let me make a suggestion. WE HAVE EVEN MORE FAITH than the Centurion. WE NEVER SAW JESUS FACE TO FACE, yet we believe. Jesus didn't pass through our town in the flesh, yet we believe. We may even be able to say we have more faith than the Centurion. We believe without seeing!

SICKNESS IS NOT CROSS TO BEAR

Luke 9:23-24

23 *Then he said to all, "If anyone wishes to come after me, he must deny himself and take up his cross daily and follow me.* 24 *For whoever wishes to save his life will lose it, but whoever loses his life for my sake will save it.*

Sickness is not a cross you have to bear. I am not sure why we grow up believing that. It may have begun as a way to comfort those who are sick or to encourage them to stick it out. Maybe it was taught to us as a way to make us feel good about being sick as though we were special and had a part in someone else's salvation. We always want to feel productive and that our lives are worthwhile especially if we have to endure an illness. We want to believe it has some purpose, some redeeming value. And it may, everything we endure has redeeming value if God is a part of it. God promises to turn everything too good for those who are following Him (Romans 8:28).

Disease is evil. God does not use sickness and disease punish His children, what father would. Sickness is part of the curse that came from disobedience. In Christ, we are free from punishment and the curse is no longer meant for us because we are "in Christ Jesus" He is our covering. Jesus became a curse for us that we might be blessed.

2 Corinthians 5:21 *God made him who had no sin to be sin for us, so that in him we might become the righteousness of God.*

Ephesians 1:3 *Blessed be the God and Father of our Lord Jesus Christ, who has blessed us in Christ with every spiritual blessing in the heavens.*

If Jesus bore our sins and our sicknesses, then I don't think He needs us or expects us to carry them. We can't. We were not made to bear such a burden. Sickness, like guilt and shame, is not a cross we can carry; we cannot stand up under it, that's why Jesus came to carry it for us. We can not remain in sin or carry the guilt and shame, which is why Jesus came to save us. The same is true about sickness and disease. Jesus came to heal us. Just like Jesus is our savior, He is also our healer.

The cross God wants us to bear is to love the unlovable (the neighbor down the street, the aunt, uncle, niece, fellow worker, boss, child). The cross God wants us to bear is to speak the Word of God to those who are lost and in sin, and bring the good news of Jesus to the world around us. Are you willing to do that? Are you willing to be persecuted for Jesus' sake? That is what a cross looks like. Jesus says in Luke "If anyone wishes to come after me, he must deny himself and take up his cross daily and follow me. The cross we take up is the cross of following him. We are to suffer and lose our life for HIS SAKE; not for the sake of suffering; not for the sake of proving how strong we are, holy we are, or faithful we are.

If you choose to carry the cross of sickness and disease because you believe it comes from God to help or teach you in some way then why go the doctor? Shouldn't we just suffer with it? Does that make sense? No, it does not make sense. Let go of that false humility that says healing is for others but not me. You are not special. We are all the same in God's eyes. All equal. All equally undeserving. We all need Jesus to save us and heal us equally.

God is not holding any sin against you. The punishment for disobedience was done away with at the cross unless you want to remain in the world God transferred you out of. The Bible says that God "rescued us from the kingdom of darkness and transferred us into the Kingdom of His dear Son" (Colossians 1:13). Your Father wants you whole, healed and living the life He has called you to live. Jesus did it all for you because you are that important to Him. He didn't do it so you could be miserable, He did it that you would have life and have it more abundantly" (John 10:10).

POWER OF THE WORD OF GOD

Proverbs 4:20 *The bible says God's word is life to those who find them and health to ones own body.*

God's word in your heart, your mind and your mouth is powerful. Read God's word and believe it, rest in His word and let it minister peace and comfort and strength to you. When we read it and declare it out loud, we are retraining our thoughts to believe the word of God which is the truth instead of what our minds have been trained to believe. The Bible says "Do not conform yourselves to this age but be transformed by the renewal of your mind, that you may discern what is the will of God, what is good and pleasing and perfect" (Romans 12:2). Our feelings are not the truth. Our diagnosis is not the truth. The word of God is the truth.

DECLARATIONS FROM SCRIPTURE

I am healed because Jesus bore my sickness
and every disease.   (Mat 8:17)

Jesus bore my pain. By his stripes, I am healed. (Is 53:4-5)

God sent forth his word and healed me.   (Psalm 107:20)

The Lord is restoring me and healing my wounds.   (Jer 30:17)

The Lord forgives all my sins and heals all my diseases. (Psalm 103:3)

He redeems me from the pit and crowns
me with love and compassion.   (Psalm 103:4)

God has delivered me from every evil.   (Mat 6:13)

Christ has redeemed me from the curse of the law.
Therefore, I have been redeemed from....   (Gal3:13)

I come in the name of Jesus against the spirit of infirmity
                                          (Luke 13:11)

God says I am the Lord who heals you.   (Exodus 15:26)

I am healed and strong because I am in the Lord and in His mighty
power. He makes me strong. He is my strength.The Holy Spirit lives in
me. Greater is He that is in me than He that is in the world.
                    (Eph 6:10, 1 Cor 3:16, 1 John 4:4)

GOD KNOWS OUR NEEDS

Matthew 6:31-33 *"Therefore do not worry, saying, 'What shall we eat?' or 'What shall we drink?' or 'What shall we wear?' For after all these things the Gentiles seek. For your heavenly Father knows that you need all these things. But seek first the kingdom of God and His righteousness, and all these things shall be added to you.*

We seek after things, such as automobiles, homes, fixtures, vacations, and hobbies. We pay for insurance, healthcare and retirement plans. We are consumed with tasks and activities, and we worry about our future. God knows what we need and promises us, that when we put Him first, we won't have to worry about anything else. If God cares about what we eat and drink and even about what we wear, how much more does He care for our health, our children, and our future?

This scripture passage is concerned with our daily, physical needs while on earth. We won't need clothes or food or even drink in heaven. God heals and provides for us now, not in heaven. We won't need provision or healing in heaven. No one is sick in heaven; no one needs anything in heaven, because, in heaven, we lack nothing and the streets are paved with gold. Healing is for us now. When God tells us He cares for us or He heals us or provides, guards, protects and remains with us, He means now, on earth, not in heaven. God's Word is for us today.

Philippians 4:19 *And my God will supply all your needs according to His riches in glory in Christ Jesus.*

If we believe God's Word and live as if it's true, we wouldn't have a care in the world. I heard this story once.

Perched on a tree branch, two birds were observing passers-by rushing from one place to another. Looking at their faces, one bird asked the other, "Why is man so full of worries and cares?" The other bird answered, "Maybe they don't have a heavenly Father like we do." *(Joseph Prince)*

Why would God let us know He cares for us and then not take care of us? "Give all your worries and cares to God, for He cares about you," God tells us in 1 Peter 5:7. Why would God tell us He forgives all our sins and heals all our diseases in Psalm 103:3 and then not do it? Why would God tell us we could ask Him for anything and then turn away from us? He won't, we just have to believe it. Not only does God care about our needs, He even cares about our desires. What is the desire of your heart? Rest assured then that if God cares about giving you the desires of your heart how much more your health.

Psalm 37:4 *Delight yourself also in the Lord, And He shall give you the desires of your heart.*

HE BORE OUR DISEASES

Matthew 8:16-17 *When it was evening, they brought him many who were possessed by demons, and he drove out the spirits by a word and cured all the sick, ¹⁷ to fulfill what had been said by Isaiah the prophet: "He took away our infirmities and bore our diseases."*

If Jesus really did take away our infirmities and if He really did bear our diseases then why do we still believe we have to put up with or live with sickness and disease? Why are people still sick? Why do we believe we have to remain sick if Jesus really did take away our sicknesses?

1.   We put up with sickness in our lives because we don't know the truth. We hear and believe the diagnosis more than the Word of God. Our faith is weak. We believe at first, but then as soon as we hear one bad report we go back to fear and worry. We have to be baptized into the Word of God. The origin of the word "baptize" means to immerse or bathe. Immerse yourself in His Word. Give yourself to Him. Call upon the Holy Spirit to guide you into the truth of God's Word and make the Word of God come alive. The Bible says that a veil remains over the Word of God until the Holy Spirit takes it away.

2 Corinthians 3:15-17 *"To this day, in fact, whenever Moses is read, a veil lies over their hearts, but whenever a person turns to the Lord the veil is removed. Now the Lord is the Spirit, and where the Spirit of the Lord is, there is freedom."*

The Holy Spirit will make the Word of God come alive and meaningful. Faith comes from hearing the Word of God.

2.   The enemy. We have an enemy that deceives us and lies and blinds us to the truth so we will remain trapped.

3.   Some believe that there is a benefit to suffering. We think we are supposed to help God save souls. Jesus is God, and He is the only one who can save us. There is only one Name by which humans can be saved, and that is the Name of Jesus. The Name above all names. Only God receives that glory. It belongs to Him alone. Jesus is Lord because He earned it when He died for us. *God greatly exalted Him "and bestowed on Him the name that is above every name, that at the name of Jesus every knee should bend, of those in heaven and on earth and under the earth, and every tongue confess that Jesus Christ is Lord, to the glory of God the Father* **(Phil 2:9-11).**

4.   Some believe we are not worthy of healing. We believe instead the lie that sickness is a price we have to pay for living a certain way.

5.   Some of us believe in fate or luck. We believe it's just a part of life; the luck of the draw. We just believe some of us are lucky and some are unlucky. When you start reading and believing God's Word, you realize that luck is not your lot. I am not governed by luck. I used to be obnoxious when people would say to me "good luck", I would say something offensive like, "I don't believe in luck," and they would look at me funny. Luck is trusting in the wind or worse trusting in a fluke or an accident. We, as children of God, have a much better hope and our hope comes with a promise. *They that hope in the Lord will renew their strength, they will soar on eagles' wings; They will run and not grow weary, walk and not grow faint* (Isaiah 40:31). Luck is what people with no hope believe in. I have hope. I believe God really does care for me, because I believe His Word is trustworthy when He says *"Cast all your worries upon Him because He cares for you"* (1 Peter 5:7). We can count on His Word. God says His Word is everlasting and will never pass away and God always honors His Word.

Healing is something you and I have to receive and accept. You have to accept and receive healing just like you have to accept and receive salvation. This is the truth. Follow me for a minute while I explain. God already provided you with healing and forgiveness. It's already been done. Both are up to us to receive. Jesus isn't making a decision whether or not to heal you. He already made that decision when he sent Jesus. The bible says that Jesus carried our sickness and disease. He took our sins at the cross and our sickness. He took all the punishment for sins including sickness. We don't have to keep it.

Why do some remain sick if Jesus healed us all?
Why do some remain unforgiven if Jesus forgave us all?

Just like some of us remain unforgiven doesn't mean Jesus doesn't forgive us. It's up to us to receive and accept His forgiveness. We can go our whole lives thinking God is punishing us for a sin he already forgave through Jesus Christ. THROUGH JESUS CHRIST we have been forgiven.

The same is true regarding healing just because some of us remain sick doesn't mean Jesus doesn't heal. It's up to us to receive and accept healing. We can go our whole lives thinking God is punishing with sickness for a sin he already forgave.

We have already been forgiven for every sin we will ever commit or have ever committed. Jesus already died. He isn't going to the cross every time we sin. He made a decision along time ago to go to the cross, and it was finished and paid for. He took the cross for you and everyo other sinner in the world that is willing to make Jesus LORD, GOD, SAVIOR, KING. We just have to go to Him for the gift of salvation and freedom.

We believe Jesus forgives. It's easier to have faith for that. He died to forgive you. That is the reason he died. If we don't receive forgiveness, than he died for nothing. The same is true for healing. He came to heal us. He came to restore us to life and not just ordinary life but abundant life (John 10:10).

What is true about forgiveness is true about healing. God forgave our sins at the cross and also healed all our diseases at the cross. God did both at the cross, and just like not everyone accepts and receives the forgiveness of Jesus, not everyone accepts and receives the healing of Jesus. Just because many are sick doesn't mean God wants them that way. It doesn't mean Jesus doesn't heal. Just like because many are sinners doesn't mean Jesus doesn't forgive, in the same way, because many are sick doesn't mean Jesus doesn't heal.

1 John 2:2

And if anyone sins, we have an Advocate with the Father, Jesus Christ the righteous; and He Himself is the propitiation for our sins; and not for ours only, but also for those of the whole world.

Do you believe Jesus took away our sins? If so then it's time to believe He took away your sickness too. Sickness is simply a punishment for sin. If the sin is gone and forgiven and now on Jesus, then so is sickness, the punishment for sin. The Bible says He forgives all our sins and heals all our diseases Psalm 103:3 (NAB)

If you are sick, I want you to know there is hope for you. You may be sick now, but you don't have to stay that way. Every time we get sick, it's an opportunity for God to be glorified when we are healed. Sickness comes, but it doesn't have to stay. Don't fret if you are sick, just know that this is an opportunity to receive healing.

> **Psalm 103** Bless the Lord, my soul;
>   all my being, bless his holy name!
> [2] Bless the Lord, my soul;
>   and do not forget all his gifts,
> [3] Who pardons all your sins,
>   and heals all your ills,
> [4] Who redeems your life from the pit,
>   and crowns you with mercy and compassion,
> [5] Who fills your days with good things,
>   so your youth is renewed like the eagle's.

I believe all that God promises us, His children. He will deliver. He told us that Jesus took our sins and our infirmities and He bore our diseases, and I believe Him. He expects us to believe Him. He gave us faith. Faith is his gift to us through the Holy Spirit. He expects us to know His Word and read His Word and believe His Word; so we can live disease free, healthy, abundant lives in him and for him. He gave us the Holy Spirit to help us and open up the word for us. We need the Holy Spirit, the giver of life, to help us. He is our companion and the source of all hope, life, healing. He will bring the word of God to life for us.

We have to take Him at His Word and believe Him more than anything else no matter how strong the symptoms are or how convincing the doctors and their reports are. We have to believe him more and stay there and not be moved off of our faith by what we are seeing or feeling.

The real question is this. Is God's Word true and if so does it pertain to you and me?

HE CONSIDERS US TRUSTWORTHY

1 Timothy 1:12-17 *Gratitude for God's Mercy. I am grateful to him who has strengthened me, Christ Jesus our Lord, because he considered me trustworthy in appointing me to the ministry. I was once a blasphemer and a persecutor and an arrogant man, but I have been mercifully treated because I acted out of ignorance in my unbelief. Indeed, the grace of our Lord has been abundant, along with the faith and love that are in Christ Jesus. This saying is trustworthy and deserves full acceptance: Christ Jesus came into the world to save sinners. Of these I am the foremost. But for that reason I was mercifully treated, so that in me, as the foremost, Christ Jesus might display all his patience as an example for those who would come to believe in him for everlasting life. To the king of ages, incorruptible, invisible, the only God, honor and glory forever and ever. Amen.*

We are all called to be part of the ministry of Jesus. He considers us all "trustworthy." We are called because of our sin and through our sin to step out. To boldly step out of our sin and imperfectness, drop that heavy coat to the floor and feel that warm love of the Father. Jesus is always calling the sinner. He does not forget about you because your sin is too great, you abandoned Him too long or your unbelief too strong. It is quite the opposite. The greater the sin, the greater glory can be shown for the abundant and ceaseless mercy of God. Do not let your sin prohibit you from receiving and accepting the love and mercy of Jesus Christ. You are why He came.

Prayer: Heavenly Father, we thank you for your abundant mercy and unending love. Thank you for sending your son, Jesus Christ, to show us that perfect love. Holy Spirit, enter into us so that we may show that same love and mercy to others. Praise God, we are ALL worthy of the promises of Christ! Amen. "Let the Church always be a place of mercy and hope, where everyone is welcomed, loved and forgiven," Pope Francis.

Additional Scripture: John 1:46, John 9:3, Matthew 9:11-13, Galatians 2:20, John 1:4 **AUTHOR Jamie McCarthy**

OBSTACLES TO HEALING

 1. **Lack of Faith** - <u>Don't let your faith be shaken</u>. Read His word today and increase your faith. Read Galatians, Ephesians, John, Acts or James, Read Psalms 34, 91, 103. Just read. When we have the Word of God as your anchor, nothing can move you; no philosophy will shake your faith in Him.

> **Colossians 2:8** *See to it that no one captivate you with an empty, seductive philosophy according to human tradition, according to the elemental powers of the world and not according to Christ.*

2. **Unforgiveness** - Is there anyone you have to forgive? Do it now. We can do all things through Christ who strengthens us. Don't let unforgiveness block what the Lord has for you. The Holy Spirit will let you know if you need to forgive someone. Don't worry about it. If he does let you know than do it. It's just a decision. It doesn't mean you have to visit them necessarily. It begins with a decision then follow the Holy Spirit. If the Holy Spirit tells you to speak to the person, you will do it. But he won't ask you to do something he isn't prepared to equip you for and go with you.

3. **Love** - *Love never fails.* ***John 15:12*** *This is my commandment: love one another as I love you.* ***John 15:17*** *This I command you: love one another.*

Love is not an option it is a command. Choose today to love. The good news is that every day is a new opportunity to love someone. Love is a decision, not a feeling. It's deliberate and purposeful. It's an action and unconditional. The bible says if you can't love your brother who you see, how can you love your father in heaven who you don't see.

> *If someone says, "I love God," and hates his brother, he is a liar; for the one who does not love his brother whom he has seen, cannot love God whom he has not seen.* **1 John 4:20**

4. **Taking communion in an unworthy manner**

1 Corinthians 11:29-30 *For anyone who eats and drinks without discerning the body, eats and drinks judgment on himself. [30] That is why many among you are ill and infirm, and a considerable number are dying.*

What does this mean? I will tell you what the Catholic Church tells us it means. "If the Corinthians eat and drink unworthily, i.e., without having grasped and internalized the meaning of his death for them, they will have to answer for the body and blood, i.e., will be guilty of a sin against the Lord himself" NAB commentary. Just maybe many of us are sick because we don't know the meaning of his death. We don't know why he came and died and rose for us. The Gospel the Bible says is this, Christ was born for us, died for us, was buried for us and rose for us. He was also whipped for us, persecuted and spit on for us. All so we could know him and what he accomplished for us. To not know means he died for nothing.

5. Worry - **Luke 12:25** *Can any of you by worrying add a moment to your life-span?*

Worry is a lack of faith. As a matter of fact, it's proof you have little faith. THINK ON THESE THINGS Paul says to the Philippians. "

Finally, brothers, whatever is true, whatever is honorable, whatever is just, whatever is pure, whatever is lovely, whatever is gracious, if there is any excellence and if there is anything worthy of praise, think about these things. **Phil 4:8**

You can change your mind and when you begin to think of good things the bad thoughts leave. You can't think of two things at one time. What are you thinking about? What are you dwelling on? We are all worriers, but now I know if fear and worry come upon me, I know I am in doubt and unbelief and I am not trusting and believing in my God. I recognize worry for the evil it is and turn away from it. I have an opportunity to turn to Him or stay in worry. Turn away from worry and start speaking out loud. Say anything, "I trust you Lord" I believe you love me and are healing me" There is so much power in your words to thwart the enemy and change your thoughts. He wants your thoughts to remain on him and in his control, and not on the devil and under the devil's control. When we worry we hand over control of our lives to the devil.

6. Fear Matthew 8:26 *He replied, "You of little faith, why are you so afraid?" Then he got up and rebuked the winds and the waves, and it was completely calm.*

When fear is present, and we embrace it and enter in, faith is far away. It is like a see-saw. One or the other is present. The opposite is also true. When faith is present, fear is far away. You can't have both; only one will rule. Which one? When you are faced with fear and it creeps in. TURN TO FAITH and watch fear disappear. It can't remain with faith just like the darkness cannot remain when you turn on the light. The light overcomes the darkness. The darkness cannot overcome the light. When you have faith, fear cannot move in and take over. Remain in faith by remaining in Him and in his word. Remain attached to the vine, Jesus and his church.

7. Complaining Numbers 21:5-6 *So the people complained against God and Moses, "Why have you brought us up from Egypt to die in the wilderness, where there is no food or water?*

How do you act when you are sick? We tend to complain and talk as if we have not even asked God to heal us. We speak as though we don't believe God has heard our prayer let alone that He is acting on it. If we truly believe God hears our prayers and is doing something about it, then we would not talk as if we are still sick and as if we are never going to be healed. Complaining gets you nowhere but sick.

Complaining is just a lack of faith.We want others to sympathize with us and feel sorry for us when we are sick, but this just keeps us sick. We have to change the way we talk and the way we think and the way we act. If you are honest with yourself and recognize that you are enjoying or flirting with sympathy, you will be better equipped to fight against it. It is a trap keeping you sick. When you want sympathy, you don't want to be well. If you use sickness as an excuse to get out of something, you have opened the door to illness.

8. Doubt James 1:6 *But he should ask in faith, not doubting, for the one who doubts is like a wave of the sea that is driven and tossed about by the wind. ⁷ For that person must not suppose that he will receive anything from the Lord, ⁸ since he is a man of two minds, unstable in all his ways.*

Doubt is what the enemy sows, and it's fuel for cancer and sickness and fear and depression and all evil. Doubt is their invitation to remain. As long as we doubt God's desire to heal us, they have free reign and are very comfortable attacking you. When doubt comes and tries to grab hold of you, LIFT UP THE SHIELD OF FAITH. The scriptures encourage us when confronted with evil or temptation to lift up the shield of faith. We can't do it alone. We can't fight doubt and fear alone. See Ephesians chapter 6:10-end. Start quoting scriptures like Psalm 91. Doubt cannot remain when you read the word of God with faith see Hebrew 4:2-3.

Doubt is shaky ground, and the devil knows he is standing on shaky ground when he spreads his doubt. Because as soon as you turn that doubt to" faith" he is wasted. He slips into the abyss. He may try to grab hold of you. But as long as faith is there he has nothing to hold on to.

I once had a vision as I was praying for a friend fighting cancer, that the cancer cells were brown and slimy and they hung on by a thread. They knew they were trespassing, but since no one was forcing them to vacate, they remained and settled in and grew. The devil is a LIAR. Cancer has no right to us whatsoever. If Jesus took cancer from us and he did, then it cannot remain.

Symptoms are lies of the enemy to get us to fear and doubt our healing. Demons hold fast to doubt. It has been revealed to me just how ugly doubt is and sinful. THIS HELPS ME. I used to let doubt run wild all the time. I just don't have enough faith I would say as if that was ok, expected, tolerated. Well, it's time for a change of heart. Jesus supplies all the faith we need. So there is an infinite supply of faith. Just turn to him and read his word. Spend time with him, and your faith will sky rocket. No excuse. There will always be temptations to doubt. If we lean on our past experiences or other's experiences and circumstances, we will doubt. The Bible says lean not on your own understanding but trust in the Lord with all your heart (Prov 3:5)

GO BEYOND YOUR REACH

Luke 5:4 *When He had stopped speaking, He said to Simon, "Launch out into the deep and let down your nets for a catch."*

Peter did as he was told, and he was amazed at the boat load of fish he caught. Go, ask, and trust for more than is physically possible and you will experience the deep and come out with a surprise, a miracle, a testimony and a witness of God's power. You won't experience God's power in the shallow end of the pool or by playing it safe. But when you are willing to go "where feet may fail" (Oceans lyrics by Hillsong United) God rewards you beyond your imagination.

Do you want more? Do you want to grow up, spiritually and experience His mighty power in your life? Launch out into the deep waters. Spread your wings, extend your reach and go where you have never gone before. Move into the unknown and go beyond your comfort zone.

A friend of mine, Sheila, did that recently when she stepped out of her comfort zone and invited friends and acquaintances to her home to share her testimony. Sheila turned her boat toward deep water and came up with a payload. She may not know it or see it yet, but God has a reward stored up for her simply because she put out into the deep.

God is drawing you out into the deep. What is keeping you on the shore? Are you afraid you can't do it? Are you unsure of yourself, or worried God won't be there? You will never know what you are capable of until you believe that, "with God all things are possible." Take the leap. Trust in His faithfulness. Trust He won't let you fall. Trust that you know God's voice. If it's not God's will for you, He will redirect you and keep you safe. Trust Him. Maybe you want to join the choir or bible study or show up at prayer group. Take courage today knowing this is God's desire for you, and He has your back.

Today is the day!!! Are you ready for God to blow you away? Try something you have never tried before. Go where you have never gone before. Ask God for something you have never asked Him for. BELIEVE like never before. Don't ask God for something that you can do. Ask Him for something that is impossible and have patience that he is bringing it to pass. If you believe and keep believing God will receive all the glory and really what is better than that. I think my life is complete if God is glorified through me. It only happens when you and I are willing to step out into the deep.

Maybe this is the day you pray in tongues for the first time. Maybe today is the day you invite the Holy Spirit to take over. You did it at confirmation now is the time to renew your confirmation and say, "Holy Spirit I invite you to have your way with me."

Luke 11:9-13 *"So I say to you, ask, and it will be given to you; seek, and you will find; knock, and it will be opened to you. For everyone who asks receives, and he who seeks finds, and to him who knocks it will be opened. If a son asks for bread from any father among you, will he give him a stone? Or if he asks for a fish, will he give him a serpent instead of a fish? Or if he asks for an egg, will he offer him a scorpion? If you then, being evil, know how to give good gifts to your children, how much more will your heavenly Father give the Holy Spirit to those who ask Him!"*

Ask Him. He is waiting for you to ask for the power of the Holy Spirit to follow Jesus and be the Christian God has called you to be.

Take the plunge.

FOUR FAITHFUL FRIENDS

Luke 5:23-24 *Which is easier, to say, 'Your sins are forgiven,' or to say, 'Rise and walk'? 24 But that you may know that the Son of Man has authority on earth to forgive sins"—he said to the man who was paralyzed, "I say to you, rise, pick up your stretcher, and go home."*

This is the story of the four stretcher bearers or four faithful friends. They took their friend to Jesus because they believed He wouldn't let them down. When they couldn't get through the front door because of the massive crowd, they were not deterred. They did not say "oh well, we did the best we could." They didn't say to their friend, "Maybe it's not God's will for you to be healed." No, they kept at it and said something like "let's go up on the roof of this house and rip it off and find a way to carefully lower him down." They did it because the health of their friend was worth whatever the cost to them. They may have said to each other "I know everyone else wants Jesus but this may be our last chance. Let's lower him right in front of Jesus so He has to stop what He is doing and touch him." They didn't think twice about interrupting Jesus, they knew He wouldn't mind and they knew their friend was important to Him as well.

What would you do? How far will you go to get your friend or loved one an audience with the King? Jesus didn't chastise them for cutting in line. He didn't scold them for thinking their friend was more important than everyone else at the meeting place. He didn't say why don't you wait your turn. No Jesus recognized the men who carried him as faith-filled friends. Jesus saw the faith of the friends and told the man on the stretcher that his sins were forgiven. He got more than he came for. He walked out of that house that day with more than just healthy legs, he was free because his friends persevered and went the distance and laid him before Jesus. In the presence of Jesus, there is healing and wholeness, forgiveness and freedom. The friends knew this and they weren't going to let anything get in the way.

Jesus healed the man but not before announcing out loud that his sins were forgiven. All his life he lived with the shame that he had done something to deserve his sickness. It was common belief that sickness was punishment for sin and it still is. We are afraid to ask Jesus, especially in front of others. We think "what if He doesn't heal me, then what will people think of me." Are you willing to ask in front of others? Are you willing to let Jesus be glorified through you or are you too afraid He won't heal you and instead leave you hopeless? God will never disappoint you. He always comes through. The friends did not doubt Jesus' ability nor His desire to heal. They had heard of Him; of how others had been healed. They knew Jesus had no favorites and that no one was unforgivable. They were so confident of the love of Jesus that they were willing to risk making fools of themselves. They had nothing to lose. The man was already considered a sinner; there was no medical help for him. He was at the mercy of his friends.

Jesus never said no. He is not going to say no to you either. Just don't give up believing. When we quit believing, we just start believing in something else. The woman with the issue of Blood in Matthew chapter 9 turned her faith from the doctors to Jesus. She wasn't ready to die. She was ready to live. Don't turn your faith from Jesus and start believing the diagnosis.

When Jesus heals us, and we receive a miracle, it is an outward sign of God's goodness, mercy, and grace. God wants to show you, and the world through you, just how merciful He is to those who believe in Him and come to Him and call on Him.

God wants you to know that your sins are not keeping you sick. God cleansed you of all your sins, so sickness has no right to or authority over you. It is punishment for sin in the Old Testament, but since Jesus took all our sins, then there is no punishment remaining. There is no reason for Jesus not to heal you. Risk believing it.

THE SPIRIT OF INFIRMITY

Luke 13:10 *Now He was teaching in one of the synagogues on the Sabbath. [11] And behold, there was a woman who had a spirit of infirmity eighteen years, and was bent over and could in no way raise herself up. [12] But when Jesus saw her, He called her to Him and said to her, "Woman, you are loosed from your infirmity." [13] And He laid His hands on her, and immediately she was made straight, and glorified God.*

I wonder if the woman in the scripture passage above knew she had an evil spirit. Jesus recognized it and set her free. He loosed her from the bondage. He laid His hands on her, and she stood up straight. I wonder how many of us are under attack and don't even know it. We may believe God is trying to teach us a lesson when in fact all along it is an evil spirit.

I wonder what the professionals called it. Surely they had a medical name for it like "Curvature of the spine" or degenerative disc disease. Maybe they diagnosed her with scoliosis, stenosis, or arthritis. I am sure this woman, after 18 years of this, never thought she would ever be free. The Bible says that

Acts 10:38 *"God anointed Jesus of Nazareth with the Holy Spirit and with power, who went about doing good and healing all who were oppressed by the devil, for God was with Him"*

What she considered a physical problem that she just had to live with, was, in fact, a demonic problem that she didn't have to live with.
Did the demons have a right to her?
What caused her to be so oppressed?
What could she have done to deserve this?
We don't know, but we do know that it was Jesus who delivered her.

We need to see cancer as our enemy. Think of cancer as the devil oppressing you and know that God sent Jesus to rescue you. I was taught to pray against the spirit of infirmity when I was growing up as a prayer leader. I looked up the word infirmity in the Bible and according to Merriam-Webster Dictionary the definition of infirmity is:

- the quality or state of being weak or ill especially because of old age

- a disease or illness that usually lasts for a long time

The woman was probably elderly. We assume so because she was sick for such a long time or maybe it's because we have seen senior men and women bent over like this. I wonder how many of the elderly sick with a disease actually have the "spirit of infirmity" oppressing them. Maybe they are waiting for one of us to notice (see) them like Jesus did.

Sometimes we look differently at the elderly. We expect the elderly to get sick as if they are supposed to. We don't seem to fight the same way in prayer for them as we may others. People think things like "At least, they have lived their life" as opposed to the child who has his whole life ahead of him. When a child becomes dreadfully ill the whole church, sometimes the whole community, becomes involved. When the sick person is older, we don't have the same passion for fighting or intervening. It's as if God has only so many people He can heal at any given time. No matter how old you are, you want to be healed. It hurts the same no matter what your age. When someone is young and pretty, we somehow think they deserve healing more than another. Thank GOD his ways are not our ways.

Jesus was different. Jesus has no favorites. Thankfully God doesn't have to pick and choose who to heal. He has the power and desire to heal anyone and everyone. He has compassion even on and maybe especially, the elderly. In Matthew chapter nine a man comes to Jesus because his young daughter is ill. Jesus agrees to visit her and on the way He stops His entourage for an older woman who had been sick for 12 years. Jesus was on His way to heal a little girl but took the time to stop and reassure and speak healing to an elderly woman.

A EUCHARISTIC MIRACLE

Hebrews 8:12 *For I will forgive their evildoing and remember their sins no more."*

This is my story of healing. It's not a story of physical healing but of emotional and spiritual healing.

Often it seems easy to pray for physical healing when you're sick. Being sick or having some sort of physical pain is out of your control. No one brings that kind of pain on themselves. When you're the cause of your hurt, it's much more difficult to ask for that healing. We think we deserve that pain. It's our way of showing remorse to God. We bring on that suffering and carry it with us as our own personal cross to bear. But that's the devil giving us those thoughts. That's not what God wants. God wants each of us to feel his forgiveness, mercy, and love. It is not his desire for us to go through life suffering, physically or emotionally.

This is the journey of how I came to accept my emotional healing.

I made some pretty terrible decisions in my college years that put me on a quick downward spiral into depression and a loss of self-respect. It was a very dark period of my life. One that I wasn't looking to get out of or thinking that I ever would. Thankfully, God had other plans for me; and, despite my best efforts to ignore him, he would bring a man into my life that would show me the forgiveness of our Father. I would marry this man; and, shortly after the wedding, begin going through the RCIA process in Plano, TX.

I can remember almost every detail of my first reconciliation. I was fairly certain that I would be excommunicated before I ever became Catholic. But God would grace me with the kindest, most compassionate and loving priest, Father Henry, as my confessor. I'll never forget how at the end of my very long confession, Father Henry took hold of both my hands, looked me straight in the eyes, and with a goofy grin on his face said, "God has already forgiven you. You just need to forgive yourself." I wouldn't listen to the advice that day. I would continue to carry that pain and guilt for many years.

After four different moves across the country, we eventually found our way back to Texas. This time living in McKinney. My oldest daughter was preparing for first communion, and it was time for her first reconciliation. I remember sitting in the sanctuary of our parish having a very long debate with myself about whether or not I would go to confession too. I hadn't been in 10 years. Not since that first confession with Fr. Henry. I was desperately trying to find a good excuse not to go. When the visiting priests came in, I was shocked to see Fr. Henry walks in. Seriously?!? After ten years and moves across the country, he walks into a completely different parish on this day. Okay God, I'm listening.

That was the day I forgave myself and accepted God's forgiveness and healing.

Two months later, I would be sitting at Mass. I went up to receive the Eucharist and was heading back to my seat when something incredible happened. I only took the Body that morning. I can't remember why I hadn't taken the Blood. I may have been sick or holding a baby. But for whatever reason, I only had the Body of Christ, and as I was returning to my seat, I felt it change. It seemed to grow inside my mouth, and it turned into a fleshy blob. I had an overwhelming earthy taste like dirt or sucking on a thumb. I almost dismissed it, thinking that I was crazy. But once I realized that it was a Eucharistic miracle, I had a huge rush of the Holy Spirit come upon me. The sanctuary brightened, and it was like I was seeing with perfect clarity. I had an overwhelming feeling of love for everyone in there. It wasn't like the love you have for a husband or even the love you have for your children. It was a powerful, pure, agape love. I remember really having to restrain myself from jumping up and interrupting Mass. I wanted to shout to everyone what had just happened and make them all realize what they were receiving. As each person was walking past, I just kept thinking how much I loved them. I didn't even know most of them, but I was silently telling them I loved them.

I had opened a door and Jesus pushed his way in. My life would never be the same. Praise God!

We have to allow ourselves to be healed. Jesus wants to heal us of all our brokenness. Whether it is physical or emotional, self-inflicted or not. Allow yourselves to be washed in forgiveness and mercy. That's the first step. We can't expect to heal ourselves. Only God can heal us. And once we let him in and allow him to do his work, our lives will never be the same.

AUTHOR   JAMIE McCARTHY

JUST BELIEVE

Mark 5:35-36 *While he was still speaking, people from the synagogue official's house arrived and said, "Your daughter has died; why trouble the teacher any longer?" ³⁶ Disregarding the message that was reported, Jesus said to the synagogue official, "Do not be afraid; just have faith*

Are you praying for something or for someone? What do you do when you hear a report contrary to your prayer? What do you do when you have doubts? Jesus says, "Just believe"? What? How can He say that? Doesn't He know the situation? Doesn't He understand how impossible the circumstances are? Who does He think He is saying, "Just believe"?

Believing is both the easiest and the hardest thing for us to do. Believing is easy because Jesus teaches us to believe like little children. He says to have the faith of a mustard seed. He says, to just believe. Believing is hard because maybe your prayer wasn't immediately answered, or your issue is just too big, or the report is too dire... Jesus is saying the same thing to you.

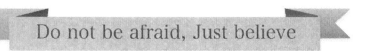
Do not be afraid, Just believe

Jesus says, for us to just believe. We have to have faith in Him. We cannot put our faith in the report or the circumstances. We have to put out faith in Jesus and in His Word. He promises to be with you, to take care of you. He is seated at the right hand of the Father interceding for you.

When fear grips you, hear Jesus speaking this to you. "Do not be afraid; just have faith" He is saying it to you lovingly and gently because he knows we are going to be afraid.

DEPRESSION

John 8:36 *"So if a son frees you, then you will truly be free."*

Depression is not yours. No matter how clinical; no matter how long it has tormented you; no matter how many doctors have diagnosed you, depression is not part of who you are. You can walk out from under depression beginning today because Jesus has already conquered it, destroyed it and removed it's ability to harm and control you. You are free because in Jesus Christ we are free and you and I are "IN CHRIST." I am not saying quit your drugs or walk away from your doctor's orders, but I am saying to believe God more.

Think of depression as an instrument from hell sent to attack you and harm you. God says that "EVERY weapon fashioned against you shall fail" (Isaiah 54:17), so depression has no right to you, and no authority over you. It's time for you to rise up with power and destroy its hold on you, and you can do it beginning today because the Bible says that the Greater one lives in you.

1 John 4:4 *You belong to God, children, and you have conquered them, for the one who is in you is greater than the one who is in the world.*

In him and connected to Him you can do all things. Nothing is too difficult for you because you are in Him and He is in You. Who? Jesus. Jesus is more powerful than anything coming against you and now is your time to reclaim your life. Jesus is the Redeemer who died that you might have life and have it abundantly. So what are you waiting for? Do you really think God wants you depressed? Do you think God is using this to teach you a lesson? That is absurd. *(John 10:10, Phil 4:13, Jer 32:17)*

Jesus went to the cross carrying all your sins and sickness and disease, the Bible says, so you can be free to live not just in heaven but now. Eternal life begins now. You have been redeemed, purchased for freedom. Thefreedictionary.com says this about the word redeemed - " to buy or pay off; clear by payment;

to *recover* ownership of by paying a specified sum." Jesus paid with his blood for our lives, your life, so start living.

We were once slaves the Bible says *"Jesus answered them, "Amen, amen, I say to you, everyone who commits sin is a slave of sin"* ***(John 8:34).*** Jesus came, the Bible says, to free us (REDEEM US) from the curse of slavery to sin. You may say to yourself. "I am not a slave to sin." You are by your very nature sinful until you come to Jesus for conversion and new life. He takes our old condition and gives us a new heart, a heart for him. The Bible says we literally become a new creation in Christ and through Christ.

2 Corinthians 5:17 *So whoever is in Christ is a new creation: the old things have passed away; behold, new things have come.*

If we don't know what Jesus did for us, we will never receive it. The devil will keep us in chains forever if we let him. If we believe we are under a curse (depression, anxiety) instead of "redeemed" from the curse (depression, anxiety)" it will continue to have power over us. Expect to grow up in the Lord. Choose life in him and with him today. Surrender your old self for the new self by giving your life to Jesus. He will transform us into his image *(2 Corinthians 3:18).*

You don't have to live with fear, depression, or anxiety. It's not your burden to carry. Now believe it. Believe more in the power of Jesus, than in the power of depression to control you and ruin your life. The Bible says that Jesus came to destroy the works of the devil *(1 John 3:8).* First, you have to see depression as a work of the devil. If you do, it's easier to believe you are free from it and don't have to be a slave to it.

DEPRESSION IS A KILLER

Psalm 103:4 *Who redeems your life from the pit, and crowns you with mercy and compassion*

Depression is a killer. It kills your will to live, your lust for life, your desire to love, your relationships, your finances, and your time. Jesus said, "*A thief comes only to steal and slaughter and destroy; I came so that they might have life and have it more abundantly* (John 10:10). This isn't your lot in life. You don't have to settle for this. If Jesus came to bring us life and not only life but the good life, then why are we still in darkness, in the pit, in trouble, drowning, and dying?

We are not living because we don't know that real life is ours in Christ. God not only sent Jesus to die for us and to take away our sins, but he also rose from the dead to bring us new life in him. This new life doesn't begin when we die but right now. God wants us to rise and live, but we are still listening and believing the liar. Our minds need to be renewed. We can't keep thinking as we have always thought, speaking like we've always spoken. We need to shake off the old and start fresh. We need to speak to ourselves and convince ourselves that we are brand new creatures, created in Christ to live in him. We are brand new, born again children of the most high God. How do I know this. The bible, which is God's word, says so.

God wants you to live starting right now. It may take some rehab so let's get started. Begin by calling on the Holy Spirit. Jesus left and went to heaven, but as soon as he got there, he sent us the Holy Spirit to help us and to guide us and to give us everything we need to live this life as a child of God in His kingdom.

Invite the Holy Spirit to show you what the word of God means. Go ahead and try it. Open up the word of God to John chapter one and begin reading. Say "come Holy Spirit, open up the word for me. Speak to me and give me ears to hear and understand."

Today is a new day. If you are depressed, sick, tired or defeated, tell yourself "Today is a new day," as part of your rehab. Begin speaking to yourself and say...

"(Your Name) rise up today and walk." Today is the first day of the rest of your life. I belong to Jesus. I am his son/daughter and depression, anxiety, you are trespassing on private property." Today is a great day. Jesus is Lord of my life. The Blood of Jesus has rescued me from the power of darkness. I am well. I am whole because Jesus made me whole."

SAY IT EVERY DAY until YOU BELIEVE IT!

The Bible says when you submit yourself to God, the devil will flee. Don't worry it **IS** happening but he is not going to give you up without a fight. Don't submit to him, submit to God. That is how you fight, your submission to God is fighting!!! The devil will do whatever it takes to get us to doubt. Don't let him win. Fight by speaking every day. Read God's word aloud every day. This is medicine and ammunition. The devil will try to convince you he still has you, but he doesn't. As long as you believe the devil and allow him to convince you that you are still trapped, you will be. Everything He does and says is a lie to try to convince you he is still in charge and has a hold of you.

DEPRESSION IS A THOUGHT - A SERIES OF THOUGHTS

Usually right after someone is healed or set free, the devil will try to take one more stand to get you to stay in doubt and unbelief; to rob you of your miracle. If you prayed and want to remain in faith, don't listen to how you feel, listen to God's word.

IF YOU ARE STILL FEELING DOWN, FEARFUL or SICK don't give up fighting. If you are being attacked and you feel the need for deliverance because you hear voices it's time to take your life back beginning today. The enemy is destroyed and has no power over you and me but the power you and I allow him to have. So today is the day you stand.

REHAB or therapy takes daily work and SO DOES THIS!!!!

"Well, I don't feel free." You are so used to feeling depressed and being depressed, and you have been lied to for so long it's hard to believe the truth. I am praying for you to receive the truth today. I believe you are not reading this by accident. Jesus wants you to know he cares for you and has a way out. Follow him and see. Try following Jesus and watch depression flee from you. It may not happen overnight. Bad thought patterns are hard to break. Think of today as your first day of rehab. You are rehabbing the way you THINK and TALK and BELIEVE. It begins with the Word of God and surrendering to Jesus. If you have never done this for yourself, do it now. *"Jesus I choose You as my Lord and Savior. I believe you died for me and purchased for me a free ticket to heaven. I accept the invitation and thank you for it. I believe you not only died for me but rose from the dead to bring me new life and I choose that new life you died and rose to give me."*

Today is the day you make a decision that this (what is coming against you - depression/sickness) is not God's will for you and accept his healing. It is yours today because you are his child and he won it for you. Begin to walk it out and get rid of the old thoughts and feelings by renewing your mind in the word of God. Just like rehab you have to do it daily. You have to retrain your body and mind to believe differently and think new thoughts. You have been conformed to the world we live in, and now it's time to be conformed to God's world, His Kingdom.

NEXT Jump out of bed and start praising GOD.

If you can, praise him for five whole minutes. Just start walking around telling God what an awesome and wonderful God he is. The devil will hate it, so do it, and faith will rise up in you. You may even begin to believe that what you are saying is true. When we magnify GOD, he becomes the great big God that He is and our problems and circumstances become small in comparison.

How do we praise God you say? Begin by opening your mouth and start speaking. "God you are my rock, my sure foundation, my God in whom I trust. You are my ever present help in time of need. You are the way, the truth and the life. You are the GOD of all god's, the Lord of all lords, the King of all kings. You are the one that makes everything right. You are my champion, my defender, and my advocate." Praise is supernatural. We will never know all that it does on this side of heaven. But heaven moves when we praise God. God commands us over and over again to praise him, not for his sake but for ours. Watch what it does for you.

If you believe God wants you to remain as you are, then you won't do this. If you believe there is hope for you with God, you will get to work on yourself. Rehabilitation. Rehab is never easy, but there are always results. Get busy "rehabbing" the way you think and believe and ultimately the way you feel. Start with your new morning exercise. Who can't start with 10 minutes a day? There is life for you, life worth living.

GOD'S WILL IS TO HEAL

So many of us end our prayers for healing for ourselves or a loved one with the phrase, "But, Your will be done, Lord." I want to suggest to you a radical thought, and that is, It is His will to heal you. Jesus said, "Ask me for anything in my name"... but then, we add the but! I know, I used to do it too. Just take it on faith that His will is to heal you. He is the giver of all good gifts. When the answer doesn't come quickly, hang in there and don't quit resting and trusting him to heal you. It's when the answer is slow to come that we are tempted to add "well it must not be God's will."

God's will is to heal. It is his will. We don't have to pray "But your will be done" We are so used to praying that, that we actually believe it is the way to end all prayer. The other day I was going to bed and started to think of my daughter, and I just began praying for her. I prayed for her protection and her job. I prayed "Father, bless my daughter and may she have a great day at work tomorrow.

If I am not convinced that God wants to heal, I will never be convinced that God wants to bless my children or me. If God doesn't heal, why would he care about whether or not my daughter has a good day at work? Why would I ever ask such a thing if he doesn't care about our health? In other words. God either blesses or he doesn't, he either heals or he doesn't. He doesn't choose to bless some of his children. He blesses all of us who are in Christ Jesus. The Bible says *"All God's promises are "yes" and "amen" in Christ Jesus"* (**2 Cor 1:20**).

We say "God is good all the time and all the time God is good. It doesn't mean anything if God doesn't heal.

Why is it so hard to believe that God's will is to heal?

COMMON REASONS we **don't** believe it is God's will to heal:

I.   It's what we have been taught. But, there is more evidence it is God's will to heal than it isn't God's will to heal. According to the Bible:

- Jesus never said no to anyone who asked for healing.
- Jesus confirms He is willing when He says to the leper in Matthew chapter 8 *"I am willing, be healed"*
- Jesus only did what the Father told him to do. John 5:19 – *"Jesus answered and said to them, 'Amen, amen, I say to you, a Son cannot do anything on His own, but only what He sees His Father doing; for what He does, His son will do also.'"*
- When Jesus teaches us how to pray He tells us in Matthew 6:10 *"may Your will be done on earth as it is in heaven."* God's will is the same on earth as it is in heaven. In heaven, there is no sickness.

II.   We don't believe we deserve it. We believe we are unworthy

- Jesus made us worthy. Jesus came to restore us to the Father. He took our sins so we can approach the Father blamelessly.
- Imagine a judge making a decision in your favor. He decides to let you go. You don't deserve to be exonerated, but this Judge has declared you free to go. Someone paid your fine, and there are no outstanding judgments against you. You are free to go. Go anywhere. You are free. There are no chains, no jail, no fines, no restrictions. This is what God did for us. The whole blame is on Jesus. He took the blame. He became the guilty party.

III.   God is using sickness to teach us a lesson

- Is that really how a good parent acts?
- Would you ever put sickness on your child?
- No, sickness is part of the fall of humankind, part of this world, but not part of God's kingdom.
- If you truly believe God is using sickness to teach you a lesson, then learn the lesson and quickly. God is not

hiding the lesson from us. Maybe you think he is punishing you. God punished Jesus for all your sins, not some of your sins all of them. There is no punishment left for those of us "In Christ." Truthfully, if you are sick, you don't want God's will unless his will is to heal you. If we really want God's will and believe that his will is for us to be sick, then why would we go to the doctor. If God wants you to remain sick to teach you a lesson then why would you work so hard to get well. Aren't you afraid of going against his will? Why take pain medicine. If God is using the pain for a reason, then don't interfere with pain killers. If God is teaching you something, then learn it fast. He is not playing "hide and seek" with us. He will reveal it to you.

IV.   God may be using our pain and sickness and suffering to save someone else and we should offer it up

- This theology is ludicrous but many teach and believe this. If God needed us sick why would He heal everyone who came to Jesus for healing? Jesus is the same today and yesterday the bible says. He hasn't changed. He is still healing. He is alive. If this were true we would believe sickness to be a noble cause and hope our children would get sick. It's preposterous to think this is God's desire. We would never pray for anyone to get well if their sickness was important to God. Why would we ever go to the doctor? Why would we ever pray to God for anything?

V.   The answer doesn't come immediately and we lose faith.

VI.   He didn't heal _____ or _____, so he must not heal.

- We aren't meant to understand everything. We don't know why some receive healing and others don't. We don't know when it's time for a person to go to heaven. God doesn't call us to understand. He calls us to believe.

Why I never use "but your will be done" regarding healing:

I.   It is His will and I have decided to always assume it is His
       will is to heal. Why assume it may not be? Have you ever
       noticed how easy it is to say, "I am dying" when you feel
       rotten. How about saying the opposite, say "I am well
       because Jesus heard my prayer and has healed me. He took
       my infirmities and carried my disease. By His Stripes, I am
       healed. Thank you, Lord, for healing me for taking this
       burden from me."

II.   **"But your will be done"** Ends prayer! How do you keep on
       praying for healing when you just prayed "but God your will
       be done?" I have finally come to the realization that the truth
       is people do not really want God's will, they want to be
       healed. If you are sick you don't want God's will unless His
       will is to heal. You don't really believe it's God's will to keep
       you sick. If you really want God's will and believe in His
       ability to perform His will why go to the doctor. If it's God's
       will that you be sick then don't go to the doctor. If God wants
       you to remain sick why go to the doctor. If you do then you
       are going against God's will

III.   We like to pray **"But your will be done"** because we are lazy
       and don't want to press in. But your will be done closes the
       prayer, ends the prayer and we get to go back to doing what
       we do. It's hard to pray and press in and remain faith-filled
       for the sake of your loved one or a fellow parishioner. It's
       hard. It's easier to say well it must be God's will.

IV.   We don't want to look foolish. What if God doesn't heal, will
       I look silly asking for something that doesn't happen. Be
       willing to look like a fool. Be willing for the sake of the sick
       person. Remember the four stretcher bearers in Luke
       Chapter 5:17-26? They were willing to go through the roof.
       They could have, and by anyone else's standards, should
       have given up and said: "Well it must be God's will." They
       were willing to look like fools. What if they did all that and
       Jesus said no!!!. Jesus never says no. They knew that. We are

so afraid of what others will think about us. We are afraid of looking bad. If I ask and God doesn't what will people think? They will think I am not holy enough.

I hope you are still reading. "Your will be done" is important just not regarding our health. SEE NEXT CHAPTER

WHEN YOU SHOULD YOU PRAY GOD'S WILL

God's will is where we want to be. Everything we do and say should center around His will for our lives especially if we want to live the good abundant life God has planned for us. We should pray God's will. When it comes it to healing though we need to know that it is already God's will. Let's put our "But Lord your will be done" into action

     When raising our children,

     Purchasing a home,

     Taking a new Job,

     Where to go on Vacation,

     Buying a car,

     Choosing what house to buy,

     How to decorate,

     What club to join,

     What television to buy,

     or Where our children should go to college.

Truthfully we do not want God's will when it comes to deciding whether or not to buy a Mercedes or a Ford. We make these impulsive and emotional decisions all the time and on our own without the help of God. We don't want him interfering because what if he tells us to buy the Ford when we. You don't want to be put in the position to go against him, so we choose not to involve him at all. Imagine how well off we would be if we did.

TESTIMONY

My van was totaled when someone ran into me at a red light, a few years back so Mark (my husband) and I began to look for another car. The first car I entertained was a Ford Escape but only briefly. I loved it but thought it wouldn't look as well as an Acura MDX in the Dowell Middle School carpool line. I spent all my efforts on the MDX and kept coming up short. Each time we would make an appt. to see it, we would arrive, and it was already gone. Hmm. We would sit in parking lots looking at cars praying "Lord don't let us make a mistake. We want your will for us. You know what we need" We would be ready to make a decision, feel no peace and leave.

Finally, one Friday morning Mark came up to me and said these words exactly. " Marybeth, I believe the reason we can't find a car is that God wants to give us one." I will never forget those words. That very evening on the way home from my son's baseball game, Mark said "Do you want to go to Nissan of McKinney? They are raffling one of their cars tonight. I said, "Oh no I have such a headache." He said, "they are giving away hotdogs and drinks." "YES"

On the way there we prayed "Lord if it's your will we are asking for favor in the raffle" I dropped Mark and David, my youngest son, off to fill out the paperwork, parked the car and caught up with David standing in line for hot dogs. When I finally got a chance to look at the car they were raffling I said: "This is my car!" "THIS IS MY CAR" It was a black Ford Escape with grey leather interior and side runners. It was perfect, and I loved it. When it was time for the raffle, they chose our name. I sobbed thanking God.

God really does care about us. It was so obviously God's intervention, that I can never doubt his love and care for me. I know he is going to provide for me and take care of me and bless me and my family always. If God cares about giving me a car, don't you think he cares about my health. If he cares about me, he cares the same about you. He has no favorites. He loves us all the same. God is a good God and a giver. Expect to receive.

BELIEVE MORE IN GOD'S WORD THAN THE BAD REPORT

Matthew 21:21-22 *Jesus replied, "Truly I tell you if you have faith and do not doubt, not only can you do what was done to the fig tree, but also you can say to this mountain, 'Go, throw yourself into the sea,' and it will be done. 22 If you believe, you will receive whatever you ask for in prayer."*

Jesus cursed the fig tree, and it withered and then he began to teach his disciples about the power of their words. He told them that they too could command the mountain to move. If they believed that the mountain would indeed move, the mountain would have to obey that person. Have you asked God for anything big lately? Have you asked for healing from cancer or some other disease? Have you moved a mountain by speaking to it?

Have you asked someone else to pray with you or to lay hands on you? Have you asked the priest or pastor to anoint you? Did you ask God to heal you of this cancer or disease attacking you? If so, do you believe something happened? Do you believe you are healed or are the symptoms still there causing you to doubt? You are not alone. It is extremely hard to have faith when the whole world believes more in cancer, and it's devastating effects than the word of God which says.

- I will remove sickness from your midst; **- Exodus 23:25**
- I am the Lord who heals you. **- Exodus 15:26**
- And the Lord will protect you from all sickness. He will not let you suffer from the terrible diseases you knew in Egypt, but he will inflict them on all your enemies! **- Deuteronomy 7:15**
- He forgives all my sins and heals all my diseases. **- Psalm 103:3**
- When it was evening, they brought him many who were possessed by demons, and he drove out the spirits by a word and cured all the sick, to fulfill what had been said by Isaiah

the prophet: "He took away our infirmities and bore our diseases." - **Matthew 8:16-17**

- He bore the punishment that makes us whole, by his wounds we were healed. - **Isaiah 53:5**
- Jesus says "Ask and it will be given to you; ....8 For everyone who asks, receives;" - **Matthew 7:7-8.**

If God says it in His word, He expects us to believe it. He expects us to believe that we are healed. He expects you to believe he heard your prayer and is working on your behalf. '

Go, throw yourself into the sea,' and it will be done. 22 If you believe, you will receive whatever you ask for in prayer." **Matthew 21:22**

Did Jesus mean it or was he just getting our hopes up? Imagine if we believed it to be true. It's especially hard to believe if you still feel sick or you still have the symptoms. Don't give up just because you feel bad. Don't give up just because you receive a bad report.

There is a battle for your faith. Stay in the battle do not quit. I want to encourage you to believe more in God and his word than what the doctors or the medical community say and teach. That doesn't mean you shouldn't go to the doctor. It doesn't mean you should stop taking your medicine or stop listening and following doctor's orders; it means that while you are going to the doctor, your faith rests in God's faithfulness and the knowledge that he has your back and will not disappoint you.

"Go," said Jesus, "your faith has healed you." **Mark 10:52**

To overcome and stand in faith, as God wants you to, takes determination and work. This work is not grueling but simply takes commitment and a little bit of time. The work is this - speaking the truth; His truth and His truth is found in His word. Watch your faith grow as you speak the truth out of your mouth. The Bible says that faith comes by hearing the word of God. So start gathering Bible verses and start speaking them so you can hear them. You will see your faith grow.

Keep reading the Word of God even when the symptoms are in your face. They are not as real as God's word. God's word is more powerful, but it takes time to grow and listen and hear and believe it. Give yourself time hearing and listening to God's word and you will begin to believe and trust God as you walk by faith and not by sight.

For we walk by faith, not by sight. **2 Cor 5:7**
Therefore I tell you, whatever you ask for in prayer, believe that you have received it, and it will be yours. **Mark 11:24**

WHEN JESUS DIED, THE OLD COVENANT DIED WITH HIM

Matthew 27:50-51 *And Jesus cried out again with a loud voice, and yielded up His spirit. And behold, the veil of the temple was torn in two from top to bottom; and the earth shook and the rocks were split.*

The veil was torn the moment Jesus died. The veil in the temple separated the people from God. The temple was originally designed by God. He gave specific instructions to Moses in the desert on how to build the tabernacle. There was a veil before the Holy of Holies that separated the Holy of Holies from the rest of the Temple. No one could enter the Holy of Holies except the High Priest and only once a year on the Day of Atonement. On that Day of Atonement, the High Priest brought with him the blood from the sacrifice (See Leviticus 16:15). That blood was sprinkled on the Ark of the Covenant and covered the sins of the people. The Ark of the Covenant was a structure made according to God's instructions and held the broken Ten Commandments, Aaron's staff and a jar containing Manna.

When God looked down on man's sinfulness, which was represented by the broken commandments, he saw the blood. The blood was the way the High Priest cleansed the temple of the sins of the people. This was done according to God's command.

"Indeed, under the law almost everything is purified with blood, and without the shedding of blood there is no forgiveness of sins." **Hebrews 9:22**

When the Israelites were enslaved in Egypt for hundreds of years, God sent the angel of death to Egypt to force Pharaoh to let his people go. The angel was sent to kill the first born of every family. Moses had every family sacrifice a lamb and put the blood of that Lamb on the top of their doors. When the angel saw the blood, he passed over that home. Hence, that night was forever remembered as "Passover" because that was the night God spared the firstborn of every Israelite family who had the blood of the lamb on their doorpost. Passover was celebrated annually to remind the people of how great their God was and to remind them of their great deliverance from slavery. We have the blood of the lamb covering us, and we too are spared because of the blood, his blood, not ours.

When Jesus died, the old covenant died with him. There was no more need for the veil or the Holy of Holies. There was now a new high priest, and he was serving at the real HOLY OF HOLIES in heaven. There was no need for the temple and the animal sacrifices anymore.

Jesus is our High Priest. He is not only the final High Priest, but he is also the final sacrifice as well. He offered himself on the altar for the forgiveness of sins forever. His sacrifice lasts forever. He is the final sacrifice, the perfect sacrifice. His blood not only covered us but cleansed us from all our sins once and for all and completely.

The veil that separated the nation of Israel from God was torn from the top down the very moment Jesus died on the cross.

The veil, many sources say, was huge. Nothing and no one but God could have torn the veil in two. The message was clear. God had a new way to himself, and that way was through his son Jesus Christ. His blood was shed for us so that we could go to the Father free from sins. The blood of goats and sheep was just a foreshadowing of God's real plan. God's plan was Jesus all along. He knew we could never keep his laws on our own. We needed him. God was making a new covenant with his people through the blood of his son Jesus. The way to God is no longer through the veil. The new way to God is through Jesus. God said so. Jesus is now the veil.

The old way is no longer necessary and no longer part of God's plan. God exposed the Holy of Holies when He tore the veil. There is no more way to God through the temple sacrifices. Jesus said right before he expired "it is finished." He is the final sacrifice. All the blood sacrifices that went on day after day, year after year, for decades and centuries is finished; no longer needed. Jesus was the perfect sacrifice, the perfect, unblemished lamb. He fit the requirements made by God and satisfied God completely. God's wrath was poured out on Jesus. Jesus took all the punishment that was due us. It was laid on him. That is why we can approach God's throne with total confidence.

Hebrews 10:19-20 *[19] Therefore, brothers, since through the blood of Jesus we have confidence of entrance into the sanctuary [20] by the new and living way he opened for us through the veil, that is, his flesh...*

Jesus is the way, the only way to the Father. We accept this as the truth because God said so and this is God's decision, his plan all along and his way. Jesus says in John 14 *"No one comes to the Father except through me."* He said, *"I am the way, the truth, and the Life."* God made Jesus Lord. Jesus is Lord because God said so. God made him Lord. Man didn't decide it God did.

Philippians 2:8-11 *he humbled himself, becoming obedient to death, even death on a cross. 9 Because of this, God greatly exalted him and bestowed on him the name that is above every name,10 that at the name of Jesus every knee should bend, of those in heaven and on earth and under the earth,11 and every tongue confess that Jesus Christ is Lord, to the glory of God the Father.*

We now have access, because of Jesus to the throne of God, in the true Holy of Holies. We go through Jesus to God. We go straight to God through Jesus. I like to list the scriptures so you know I am not making this up. God says this, not me.

Romans 5:2 says "Because of our faith, Christ has brought us into this place of undeserved privilege where we now stand, and we confidently and joyfully look forward to sharing God's glory (NLT)
Ephesians 2:18 says "for through him we both have access in one Spirit to the Father" both meaning Jews and gentiles alike.
Ephesians 3:12 In him and through faith in him we may approach God with freedom and confidence.

There are other ways to God but only one sure way. Without Jesus, our confidence is in ourselves, or in our own goodness, or our obedience to the laws. We will always fail. Our confidence will be weak at best always wondering, never sure if God heard us. Because of Jesus, I can enter into God's presence boldly and with confidence because Jesus made a way and took away all my sins completely and forever.

Not only can enter God's throne room but we do so confidently. We can approach God confidently because we trust completely in Jesus' offering. We believe he died for us and was buried and took our sins with him. We go confidently because we believe our sins have been forgiven and washed away.

There is nothing keeping us from GOD!!! Jesus destroyed everything that kept us from God; everything that came between us and God the Father. Jesus made us brothers and sisters in him, and we can run to our Father in confidence and joy and peace all because of Jesus.

Hebrews 10:14
For by one offering he has made perfect forever those who are being consecrated.

Hebrews 10:35
So do not throw away your confidence; it will be richly rewarded.

Hebrews 3:1
Therefore, holy brothers and sisters, who share in the heavenly calling, fix your thoughts on Jesus, whom we acknowledge as our apostle and high priest.

Hebrews 4: 15-16
For we do not have a high priest who cannot sympathize with our weaknesses, but One who has been tempted in all things as we are, yet without sin. Therefore, let us draw near with confidence to the throne of grace so that we may receive mercy and find grace to help in time of need.

DO YOU BELIEVE I CAN MAKE YOU SEE

Matt 9:28-29 *They went right into the house where he was staying, and Jesus asked them, "Do you believe I can make you see?" "Yes, Lord," they told him, "we do." Then he touched their eyes and said, "Let it be done for you according to your faith."*

The Blind men knew Jesus as the Son of David. This is a Messianic title. God made a covenant with David that his kingdom would endure forever. Did they know who Jesus was? Maybe. Maybe many wondered. "who else could heal the blind, deaf, lame? Who else could raise the dead? Who else could speak to the wind and the waves?" Word sure got around about Jesus. I bet they heard about him all the time. "You should have seen what he did." "You should have been there, maybe he will heal you?" Well now was their chance, Jesus was walking right by them. They would not let this opportunity pass without getting noticed. They got Jesus' attention, and Jesus asked them "Do you believe I can make you see?

Why did He ask them, "Do you believe I can make you see?" I wonder if he was just giving them a chance to express their faith in him. I know he had a purpose. Jesus always does. He wants us to be partners in his great work. What a privilege. We ask and Jesus answers us but sometimes we need to come alongside him and have faith. Our words express our faith. Let Jesus know what you believe. Say it. Jesus wants to hear you, he wants to know you believe in him.

SAY THIS, you may not believe it at first but the more you say it the more you will believe it.

"I believe that I am well, I may not feel well, but I walk by faith, not by sight, faith that Jesus took my sickness and disease with him on the cross. I am strong in the

Lord and because His mighty power is in me. The greater one lives in me, and my body, muscles, nerves, tissue, organs and all my systems are healed and whole and in good working order because I have faith in the name of Jesus. My body is healed, and well and pain is leaving me because it must obey the word of God and because I come against it in the name of Jesus. Just like the police officer can command you because he does so in the name of the law and the government that supports him, so can we come against evil in the name of Jesus.

The Bible says that God "*gives strength to the fainting and he makes vigor abound for the weak and though young men grow faint and weary not so those who trust in the Lord. Those who hope in the Lord will renew their strength and will rise up on wings like the eagle's*" Isaiah 40. I am your precious child, and my hope is in you Lord. I trust you, and I believe my strength is being renewed, and I will run and not grow weary."

IS THE MOUNTAIN STANDING OR YOUR FAITH STANDING

Mark 11:22-24 *"Have faith in God," Jesus answered. Amen, I say to you, whoever says to this mountain, 'Be lifted up and thrown into the sea,' and does not doubt in his heart but believes that what he says will happen, it shall be done for him. ²⁴ Therefore I tell you, all that you ask for in prayer, believe that you have received it and it shall be yours.*

Is the mountain still standing or is your faith standing? Are you saying or speaking to the mountain? What will it take to get you to "say to that mountain.?" What will it take for you to start speaking? I know how hard it is to start, but once you start, the Holy Spirit takes over and helps you. You won't see the mountain move until you start speaking to it; until you have faith enough to command it to move.

When you "think" you are speaking to yourself. All day your thoughts speak to you. What are you saying about yourself or your situation? Do you keep reminding yourself about how big and terrible the mountain is? Do you let the mountain influence your thoughts and words? Does the mountain rule? Is it firmly in place? What do you think about this mountain? Do you tell it every day how great and powerful it is by your fear of it? Do you say silly things like "I am so sick, I am going to die? I am never going to get well?" These thoughts and words keep the mountain forever looming and victorious. It has you right where it wants you, under its thumb, in its shadow.

Some thoughts are not yours and come from the world or memories or are habitual thought patterns. Some thoughts are just demonic to get you to go where you shouldn't go in your thoughts. We all recognize those thoughts but sometimes we recognize them after it's too late and we are already in the pit of despair or hatred or bitterness.

How do we take our mind off of the mountain? How do we move the mountain or crush and destroy the mountain? Our mouth is what changes our thoughts. When we start speaking the truth, the thoughts will follow, our feelings will follow, our attitudes will follow, and faith will grow. It is that simple and yet so hard. I remember a doctor friend told me, regarding a hernia I had at the time, that and I didn't need to rush to a surgeon. He told me to give God the opportunity to heal me. For two years I kept telling myself I needed to find some scriptures and repeat them to myself. I wanted to begin praying in faith for healing. Two years later I had emergency surgery on the hernia. I look back and wonder how things may have been different if I had actually prayed about it, asked God about it, and asked my prayer partners to help me. If only I had believed God wanted to heal me. What if I had begun speaking like I am challenging you to do today. God would have been glorified. Everything we go through is an opportunity for God to be glorified.

Have you ever noticed how easy it is to complain and say " I am so sick" or "I am dying." Try the opposite. You aren't dying, but the words come out because it's an old habit. Say instead "I am alive and well." I know it doesn't feel like you are alive and well but if you are praying and trusting your health to God, then you aren't lying. It's true. You are simply believing and acting on God's word which says "All that you ask for in prayer believe that you will receive it and it shall be yours" Mark 11:24. This is how we walk by faith. Believe that what you have asked God for is already yours. You walk by faith when you speak as if you believe it's already done. We walk by faith, not by sight (2 Cor 5:7).

When you say I am well, what you are really saying is "God heard my prayer and is working on my behalf, and I believe him." God says our faith pleases him!!!

Hebrews 11:6 *But without faith it is impossible to please Him, for he who comes to God must believe that He is, and that He is a rewarder of those who diligently seek Him.*

Old habits die hard. It is going to feel weird speaking correctly after all these years, but you can do it. I have changed the way I speak so much so that I can never say " I am sick" anymore. I don't want to give sickness any excuse to stay, and I definitely do not want to invite it in. Never lie about your health. Never try to take a sick day when you aren't sick. Never use it as an excuse to get out of something. Never invite the spirit of infirmity.

Our words, remember, are powerful, and I just may get whatever it is I am proclaiming. The Israelites were given exactly what they were proclaiming when they complained in Numbers chapter 14. They complained to Moses saying something like "we are going to die in this desert; we will never make it." God made sure they got exactly what they expected to get and spoke about.

So quit saying things like " I am dying." Say the opposite " I am well, I am healthy" You may not feel well, but we do not walk by sight or by feelings but by faith.

Complaining opens the door to demonic activity, it's an invitation to make your life miserable. Demons recognize the lack of faith, and they know they are allowed anywhere doubt remains. Complaining proves we are doubting every time. The devil loves it when we complain because these complaints reassure them of our doubt and their influence on us. They rule and reign where doubt remains. As soon as they hear you proclaiming God's truth, they will try to persuade you to remain in doubt. It's easy in the beginning. But the longer we keep proclaiming God's word our doubt grows weak, and their influence weakens.

MAKE A DECLARATION OF FAITH. Don't wait till you feel it or see. There is no need for faith then.
MAKE A DECLARATION THAT YOU ARE FREEDOM. Don't wait till your are free to start declaring.
MAKE A DECLARATION THAT YOU ARE HEALED. Don't wait for the symptoms to leave.

In the middle of the revolutionary war with Great Britain, the Thirteen American Colonies governed by the Continental Congress declared their Independence. We had been at war for over a year already. The Congress announced to the world that the Thirteen American Colonies were now the Thirteen United States of America, independent and sovereign and no longer attached to the British Empire. The Continental Congress was a convention of delegates from the Thirteen Colonies which governed the United States during the American Revolution.

We declared independence then fought for it. Declaration is the beginning. We remember the day of our Declaration of Independence. We may not remember the day the war ended, but we do remember the day we declared it. That is the day we truly won. That is the day worth remembering. That is the day we made a decision and stood on it and were willing to fight for it.

What do you need to declare over or about your life? I declare I am a wife; I am a mother. I declare I am forgiven and free from all my past sins. I declare I am a student a graduate of Economics. I declare I am healthy and free from _____ .

What do you want for yourself in 5 years? Declare it now. The United States of America was still under attack and dominated by Britain, but that didn't deter them from declaring freedom and independence. Declare your independence from medicine from drugs, from cigarettes, alcohol, or from overeating. Don't worry that you are still smoking; declare it anyway.

God's Word says that "By his stripes, I am healed." God's Word says that Jesus carried our sins and sicknesses with him to the cross." God's Word says "He forgives all our sins and heals all our diseases." God's Word says that whoever says to this mountain 'Be lifted up and thrown into the sea,' and does not doubt in his heart but believes that what he says will happen, it shall be done for him. 24 Therefore I tell you, all that you ask for in prayer, believe that you will receive it and it shall be yours."

Start speaking "I am forgiven, I am free, I am loved." Say "I am his chosen one, I am the righteousness of God in Christ Jesus, I am in Christ, I am hidden in Christ, all my sins are forgiven, I am fearfully and wonderfully made. I can do all things through Christ who strengthens me. I am healed, by his stripes, I am healed, I am walking in faith and victory. Depression, I command you off of me, and I cast you by the power of the Holy Spirit in me to the foot of the Cross. I am alive and well and strong in the Lord. I have defeated the enemy, and he is under my feet. I am the head and not the tail; God has raised me up and lifted me high above my enemies."

Is the mountain still standing or is your faith standing? Which? Is Goliath still alive or dead?

The battle may be raging, but the war has been won. Have you made your declaration of independence?

HAVE YOU MADE YOUR DECLARATION OF FREEDOM; YOUR DECLARATION OF HEALTH?

FAITH

Hebrews 11:1 *Faith is the realization of what is hoped for and evidence of things not seen.*

This is the Bible's definition of Faith, and this verse is the only place we see it defined. The Dictionary definition of faith is "complete trust or confidence in someone or something."

The Bible says that faith is total confidence in something you can't see, taste or feel but is completely real. The bible says it is the realization of what is hoped for. Faith is a reality based on knowledge and understanding that defies our natural senses. We just plain know and are in complete assurance even though there is no physical proof. We know God's word is true because we just know. We are the physical proof that God exists, we his people and our faith in him because signs and wonders follow us. We prove God is real through our faith in him. Our faith is the only proof the world will ever have of God's existence. Our job, our privilege is to manifest God's presence in this world. We prove God is real by our faith in him. We make the eternal come to life physically by our faith. Our faith is the evidence of the things not seen. What is your faith evidence of?

The Bible definition of faith is difficult to understand but Paul is about to make very clear, just what faith is in Hebrews 11.

Faith is - Noah building a ship in the middle of dry land.
Faith is - Abraham offering Isaac as a sacrifice to God.
Faith is - Moses choosing the life of a slave.
Faith is - walking across the red sea between two walls of Water.
Faith is - walking around Jericho for seven days.

Paul goes on to say, "Through acts of faith, Gideon, Barak, Samson, Jephthah, David, Samuel, the prophets. . . . toppled kingdoms, were protected from lions, fires, and sword thrusts, turned disadvantage to advantage, won battles, and routed alien armies. Women received their loved ones back from the dead.

There were those who, under torture, refused to give in and go free, preferring something better: resurrection. Others braved abuse and whips, and, yes, chains and dungeons. They were stoned, sawed in two, put to death at sword's point; they went about in skins of sheep or goats, needy, afflicted, tormented." All because of faith **(Hebrews 11:32-38)**.

WOW! Every time we die to our own comfort or will or our right to be right, we are choosing something better. Resurrection from the dead! Every time we choose to die to our own needs and desires over someone else's we choose resurrection. My friend told me one day "I am looking forward to the opportunity to die to myself and be united with Him." She was talking about her future plan to love the unlovable person in her life. To humble herself for God's sake if not for theirs. She made a decision to love someone in her life who hurt her, knowing that the next time she saw him was an opportunity to bless God by dying to herself, her pride and choosing God's way. She knew though it had to start now with her thoughts. She decided to quit dwelling on what he did to her and his inexcusable behavior. She decided to quit letting it play in her mind over and over again. It wasn't going to rule her or bring her down or cause feelings of anger and hurt to rise up in her. She was choosing God's way for HIS SAKE.

2 Corinthians 5:7 *"For we walk by faith, not by sight."*

We pray, we help, we teach, we talk and live by faith not by sight. We don't pray for others to God because we see him, we pray to him because we know he is there. We don't know because of a feeling or a vision, necessarily, we know because we have had an experience or encounter, or because we have seen the evidence of God's existence and His love through others. He has made himself known to us. Some of us haven't had the encounter yet but are walking in faith believing because of what other's have taught us. Jesus said *"Blessed are those who have not seen and have believed"* **(John 20:29)** Every time you believe, God provides the evidence. You are the evidence. Your faith is the evidence that God exists. We are the body of Christ.

The unseen world is more real and permanent than the seen world. The Bible says that heaven and earth will pass away, but God's word lasts forever. What should we be spending our time, energy and money on? It makes good sense to invest in what lasts forever.

2 Corinthians 4:18 *"We look not to what is seen but to what is unseen; for what is seen is transitory, but what is unseen is eternal."*

Romans 8:24 *For in hope we were saved. Now hope that sees for itself is not hope. For who hopes for what one sees?*

FAITH IS NOT A RELIGION - CRHP

"Christianity did not begin with a theological formulation, a set of laws, or even a prayer form, it certainly did not begin with a document. It began with a person. Christianity is all about commitment to a person. The person of Jesus Christ. Jesus says, Here I am, I stand at the door and knock if anyone hears my voice and opens the door, I will come in. The act of commitment is a prayer of self-offering which in simple terms expresses belief in Christ as Savior and Lord, acknowledges our sinfulness and need and clearly places our entire life in the hands of Jesus." Christ Renews His Parish *(CRHP)* Manual

The manual goes on to say this " Being a follower of Jesus is not a matter of birth, but of decision....The tradition of infant baptism claims the faith of the community for the infant, but expects each individual to choose Jesus for himself when he is able to do so."

Charles Blondin, a famous French tightrope walker, was the first person to walk across Niagara Falls on a tightrope. After crossing it once, he asked the crowd, "Do you think I can do it again?" "Yes! Yes! Do it, Do it!" they cried. Blondin again asked his audience "Do you believe I can cross the Falls pushing a wheelbarrow? "YES!!" The crowd of over 25,000 roared in response. "We believe you can they shouted" and he did it. After reaching the opposite shore, with the crowd going crazy, he asked, "Do you believe I can do it again only this time with someone in the wheelbarrow?" THE crowd was mad with excitement and anticipation. They shouted "yes! YES! We believe!" He pointed to a man in the crowd "Do you believe? Yes, the Man shouted back. "You are the greatest in the world! I know you can!" Blondin said, "Get in."

Do you really believe or do you just get caught up in the excitement? The Bible says that faith without works is no faith at all. We prove our faith by our willingness to get into the wheelbarrow or go out on a limb. We manifest God on the earth through our faith. We make him know through our faith. We are his body speaking on his behalf, his ambassadors. We speak of him because we believe in him. We pray for other's because we know he hears us.

WHERE IS YOUR FAITH? Part 1

Matthew 8:26 *He said to them, "Why are you terrified, O you of little faith?"*

Every time I worry, it reveals my lack of faith.

We say this all the time. "Just let it go." It's almost unbearable to hear. It sounds to me so condescending. I hate hearing it because it reflects for me, my lack of faith and my pride gets injured when someone says to me "let it go." I like to be thought of as faithful or full of faith. Don't we all. Jesus recognizes our faith, so we all want to be found faithful and ready and trusting. Jesus takes such joy in our faith. Our faith pleases him, and he rewards our faith. But every time we worry we expose our lack of faith. Every time we get afraid we expose ourselves and our weaknesses.

The fact is that you and I have a whole lot of "LACK OF FAITH" and it's okay to admit it because when we recognize it, we can work on it. Our lack of faith is not the end. It's just temporary. Our lack of faith is not condemnation but a wake up call. Jesus told his disciples and even Peter about their lack of faith not to hurt their feelings or rub it in, but to encourage them to get faith. The same is true for us. The good news is your faith is lacking. That is good news; It gives me great joy to know it's just my lack of faith because that means I just need more faith. YEAH!! and who doesn't need more faith.

If God says to us "where is your faith?" That is a good thing, not a bad thing. It just shows us what we need. It lets us know there is an answer for what we are going through; we just need more faith. YEAH GOD! We have the answer. How arrogant to think we have enough faith. Faith comes, the Bible says, by hearing his word. So go and get more faith. Faith will grow as we spend time with him and his word.

The apostles in the boat heard those same words. The storm was horrendous, and they all thought they were going to die. WAKE UP JESUS!!! They found Jesus asleep in the stern, and they woke him and begged him to save them. They were sure they were going to drown, and Jesus said: "where is your faith?" So every time you are tempted to say "I am going to die; I am so sick......" just hear Jesus saying to you "where is your faith?"

Just how important is faith? How important is it to God that we have faith? The Bible says that without faith, it is impossible to please him.

Hebrews 11:6

6 But without faith it is impossible to please Him, for he who comes to God must believe that He is, and that He is a rewarder of those who diligently seek Him.

What does Jesus say about Faith? I wonder if we realize just how important faith is for healing. Read these and notice just how many times Jesus says "where is your faith?" or how many times he recognizes a person's faith for healing.

(**Matthew 6:30**)...will he not much more provide for you, O you of little faith?

(**Matthew 8:10 - healing centurion's servant**)...."Amen, I say to you, in no one in Israel have I found such faith.

(**Matthew 8:26 - storm at sea**) He said to them, "Why are you terrified, O you of little faith?"

(**Matthew 9:2 - paralytic**) And there, people brought to him a paralytic lying on a stretcher. When Jesus saw their faith, he said to the paralytic, "Courage, child, your sins are forgiven."

(**Matthew 9:22 - woman with the issue of blood**) Jesus turned around and saw her, and said, "Courage, daughter! Your faith has saved you."

(**Matthew 9:28**) Jesus said to them, "Do you **believe** that I can do this?" "Yes, Lord,"

(**Matthew 9:29 - blind man**) Then he touched their eyes and said, "Let it be done for you   according to your faith."

(**Matthew 13:58**) And he did not work many mighty deeds there because of their lack of faith.

(**Matthew 14:31 - Peter walking on water**) Immediately Jesus stretched out his hand and caught him, and said to him, "O you of little faith, why did you doubt?"

(**Matthew 15:28 - Canaanite's sick daughter**) Then Jesus said to her in reply, "O woman, great is your faith! Let it be done for you as you wish." And her daughter was healed from that hour.

(**Matthew 17:20 - boy with demons**) He said to them, "Because of your little faith. Amen, I say to you, if you have faith the size of a mustard seed, you will say to this mountain, 'Move from here to there,' and it will move. Nothing will be impossible for you."

(**Matthew 21:22**) Whatever you ask for in prayer with faith, you will receive."

(**Matthew 21:21**) Jesus said to them in reply, "Amen, I say to you, if you have faith and do not waver, not only will you do what has been done to the fig tree, but even if you say to this mountain, 'Be lifted up and thrown into the sea,' it will be done.

(**Matthew 26:33**) Peter said to him in reply, "Though all may have their faith in you shaken, mine will never be."

(**Mark 9:23 - boy with evil spirit**) Jesus said to him, "'If you can!' Everything is possible to one who has faith."

(Mark 9:24) Then the boy's father cried out, "I do **believe**, help my unbelief!"

(**Mark 5:36 - daughter died**) Jesus said to the synagogue official, "Do not be afraid; just have faith."

(**Mark 10:52 - blind man**) Jesus told him, "Go your way; your faith has saved you." Immediately he received his sight and followed him on the way.

(**Mark 11:23**) Amen, I say to you, whoever says to this mountain, 'Be lifted up and thrown into the sea,' and does not doubt in his heart but **believe**s that what he says will happen, it shall be done for him.

(**Mark 16:17-18**)These signs will accompany those who **believe**: in my name they will drive out demons, they will speak new languages. They will pick up serpents [with their hands], and if they drink any deadly thing, it will not harm them. They will lay hands on the sick, and they will recover."

(**Luke 17:6**) The Lord replied, "If you have faith the size of a mustard seed, you would say to [this] mulberry tree, 'Be uprooted and planted in the sea,' and it would obey you. The attitude of a Servant.

(**Luke 17:19 - healing of the leper**) Then he said to him, "Stand up and go; your faith has saved you."

(**Luke:18:8 - persistent widow**) But when the Son of Man comes, will he find faith on earth?"

(Luke 18:42 - blind beggar) Jesus told him, "Have sight; your faith has saved you."

(John 4:50) Jesus said to him, "You may go; your son will live." The man **believe**d what Jesus said to him and left.

(Acts 3:16) And by faith in his name, this man, whom you see and know, his name has made strong, and the faith that comes through it has given him this perfect health, in the presence of all of you.

(Acts 14:9) He listened to Paul speaking, who looked intently at him, saw that he had the faith to be healed,

HEALING TESTIMONY - (WHERE IS YOUR FAITH? part 2)

Hebrews 10:39 *We are not among those who draw back and perish, but among those who have faith and will possess life.*

We are so afraid to reference our faith and especially our lack of faith when it comes to healing. We are afraid of being offensive and hurting someone's feelings. Jesus wasn't. He was more concerned about the truth and their welfare than hurting their pride or offending them. At times, Jesus was downright offensive. He will do what it takes and say what it takes to teach us and grow us up

AS SOON AS YOU PRAY A PRAYER your faith is tested and doubt creeps in. The evil one hates your faith because it is the manifestation of God's power on earth. He hates you and your faith and will do whatever it takes to destroy it, so don't be surprised when things grow worse after you pray instead of better. It may be his last ditch effort to get you to doubt. His voice will become louder especially right before your breakthrough. Don't be easily moved away from your position of faith.

God will never say you prayed too much or for too long. God will never reprimand you for having too much faith. He did, however, rebuke his disciples on numerous occasions for their lack of faith. I don't think it's possible to have too much faith. God never says to us you should have given up sooner, why did you pray so hard? It never hurts to have faith and it never hurts to encourage someone to have faith.

You will never give someone false hope. Don't ever worry about that. God won't allow that. If you are praying God is working. You just have to believe it. God would never allow someone we are praying for to get their hopes up for nothing. We can never give someone too much hope. God will not allow your prayers of faith to go unanswered. You will see God minister to you or to someone you are praying for, as you pray. God will not leave them or you feeling lost. Praying for someone is always good and never in vain. You are making a difference. It's the devil's voice which says, "don't sow false hope" or "what if God doesn't?"

Faith, my dear friends, is believing God will. Faith is not believing God can, but believing God will. Anyone can believe God can. It doesn't require faith to believe God can!!!! It doesn't. You will be hard pressed to find a Christian who doesn't believe God can heal. We don't doubt he is able. We don't doubt his ability to heal. We do, however, doubt his desire and willingness to heal. It doesn't require faith from us to believe God can; even the devil believes God can and knows God can. It does, however, require faith to believe he will. So today is the day to believe God like never before and to have faith.

We are stretcher bearers. The stretcher bearers in Luke chapter five didn't get tired of holding their lame friend up. They didn't quit. No! Find more faith, read the scriptures on healing over and over again to equip you. Whenever I go pray for someone in the hospital, I always begin by reading the scriptures to increase my faith. I have to do this daily to wipe out the screams of this world and the devil sowing doubt and to lift myself up. Read them to yourself and those you are about to pray for. Invite the Holy Spirit to open up the word to you.

I remember when I prayed with a nurse friend of one of my prayer partners. We prayed for her healing at the hospital where she worked, and I will never forget watching faith rise up in her as we read through the Bible passages. The next day or two I received a call from my friend saying something like ..." it didn't work she has to go to MD Anderson right away, as a matter of fact, they left for Houston this morning. They may have to take her leg."
I remember hearing those words over and over "it didn't work." I knew God always worked. I prayed and sought the Lord, and He told me to get her cell phone number and call her and tell her this "It's not over." How scary, what if I am wrong I thought. What if I really didn't hear from God and it's only my imagination. I did call her, and I told her " The Lord told me to tell you It's not over" When she got to MD Anderson they found nothing, no cancer and sent her home.

Believe more in God than whatever anyone else is telling you and be willing to step out in faith.

JESUS IS THE GREAT EQUALIZER

Matthew 13:58   *And He did not do many miracles there because of their unbelief.*

I don't know about you, but I want to see God work many miracles in my life, in my family, in my neighborhood. I sure don't want to get to heaven and be from the area of the world where God did not work many miracles. I sure don't want it to be because of MY lack of faith. Our lack of faith is this. We just don't believe God wants to heal us. But consider this. God either wants to heal us or he doesn't. There is no maybe with God. He does, or he doesn't.

God doesn't have favorites. He doesn't choose one of his children over the other. So God heals all of us or he heals none of us. I know, I know this is just too hard to believe, isn't it. Maybe too good to be true would be another way of saying it. We are all the same in the eyes of God. How are we all the same? We are all the same because we were all baptized into Christ Jesus. We all come to the Father through Christ Jesus our Lord and Savior who makes us one in him, one body of Christ.

Jesus is the equalizer. There is a saying " God created man - Sam Colt made them equal" referring to the Colt revolver. Jesus is the true equalizer. In him, we are made equal; we are all the same in Christ. No matter what our past, we all become part of the same body, members of one another. Some of us are weak, some strong, but all equally loved.

Jesus covers us with his blood, cleansing us just like the high priest did in the old testament on the Day of Atonement when he entered the Holy of Holies with the blood offering. The high priest sprinkled the blood of the animal sacrifice on the Ark of the Covenant to purify the inner sanctuary of all the sins of the Israelites. When we come to God through Jesus, God doesn't see our old sinful nature he sees us sprinkled with the blood of Christ.

Because of Christ, we are justified and free from sins because we have been washed in the blood of Jesus.

Just like the Temple and Tabernacle of the Old Testament was sprinkled with the blood of the sacrifice to heal and save the people from their sins, so is this temple - YOU and ME. We are the temple of the Holy Spirit. We are where God chooses to live, and he has cleansed us with the blood of Jesus. Without the blood of Jesus, there is no home for him in us.

So if God doesn't pick and choose who gets healing and who doesn't the question is, does God heal at all? If so, healing is yours, your covenant gift. Jesus says to us "where is your faith?" not to condemn us but to encourage us that faith is ahead of us. Faith is in our future.

We are always doubting God's desire to heal us. If we are unsure of his desire, we will never have the faith to be healed. We will always doubt. We will never believe we are worthy. We will always fall short. There is always something we have done or a past lifestyle or choice we made that justify's sickness. If healing is based on our goodness, we will never deserve it and therefore never receive it. Thankfully healing comes to those who believe, no matter what their past says about them; no matter what the devil accuses them of.

In the gospels, I challenge you to find one instance where Jesus turned someone down who came to him asking for healing. He never turned anyone away, and he won't turn you away either. Just don't give up believing. It may just take a little faith and patience. *We do not want you to become lazy, but to imitate those who through faith and patience inherit what has been promised* (Hebrews 6:12). God promises to heal us in his word. Psalm 103 says He forgives all my sins and heals all my diseases 4 He redeems me from death and crowns me with love and tender mercies.5 He fills my life with good things. My youth is renewed like the eagle's!

RESIST THE DEVIL AND HE WILL FLEE

James 4:7 *So submit yourselves to God. Resist the devil, and he will flee from you.*

Do not give in to the devil, do not be manipulated or toyed with, instead submit yourself to God, resist the devil and he will flee from you.

I remember hearing this story once. One of the fathers of the faith woke up in the middle of the night. Lucifer himself was in his room when he woke up with a start, saw the devil and said "Oh, it's just you, greater is He that is in me than he that is the world" and went back to sleep. When we know that the greater one is living in us, we will not worry about the devil or his tactics. The devil is defeated and it happened at the cross. You just have to know it and wield the sword of the Spirit which is the word of God.

The devil wants us to feel bad, feel down and feel as if no one loves us. He wants us aggravated, hateful, resentful, bitter and fearful. Just recognizing him is half the battle.

Pam Criss (my dear friend) is always reminding us to recognize the devil and his tricks for what they are. He wants us confused, upset with each other and out of unity. "He wants us thinking his thoughts," she says, "so we are annoyed, full of hate, and anger in order to isolate and distract us and keep us from God." When you allow those thoughts, you are giving glory to the enemy and allowing him to win and keep you off course. The devil wants us obeying his thoughts, the thoughts he is placing in our heads and he wants us following him.

Don't give in to a bad day. No! Turn that day around by the words you let come out of your mouth. Your words will turn your thoughts. RECOGNIZE who is working on you and you will not want to give him any ground or any wins. When you realize it is the devil taunting you, you will rise up and fight. The key is knowing who is behind your bad day. Just recognize the devil and smile and say "not today! You thought you could win and own me and control me, but I know your tactics. I will run to the one who can bring me out." God will bring you out. You can't do it yourself.

Keep talking, there is power in our words. Say out loud "Today is the day the Lord has made. I will rejoice because I believe God loves me and has something good for me today. He is not disappointed in you at all - ever. He knows you better than anyone and he still loves you and believes in you. He is doing a work in you, and he is bringing it to completion. You wouldn't still be reading this if it weren't true. As you fall asleep tonight, know that he never sleeps and is watching over you. You may be having a rough day but tomorrow is a new day. He is a good father and he is not going to let you go to bed without a goodnight kiss. Let him kiss you goodnight. Let his word be the last you hear every night.

The devil wants you to focus on him and focus on your trouble instead of God because he knows good things are coming your way and he doesn't want you receiving them. He knows about tomorrow, and how it is new and God's mercy is brand new every day, so he will do his best to keep you in this day, this torment.

TAKE TIME FOR HIM TODAY -

Find a Bible and open it up, just for 5 minutes. Read John 14, 15 and 16. Read Ephesians 1, 2 and 3. Read about how much God loves you in Matthew 6:25-end and Matthew 7, 8 and 9. Read John Chapter 1, or Acts chapter 3. Psalm 95, 14, 103 or 91. Invite the Holy Spirit. Ask him for a new attitude or a new mood. Just remember the devil is working hard so good must be right around the corner. Put a smile on your face and say, DEVIL, you aren't going to win. I will not glorify you.

RESIST - REJECT - REBUKE

Luke 10:19   *"Behold, I have given you authority to tread on serpents and scorpions, and over all the power of the enemy, and nothing will injure you.*

Jesus gave us power over all the power of the enemy. Let's use it. Jesus did not leave us defenseless or powerless, but he left us powerful because the Spirit of God lives in us and this power is the same power that raised Jesus from the dead. YOU HAVE POWER over ALL the power of evil the bible says. You should never be afraid of anything the devil throws your way because the Greater one lives in you. Don't let images from the television or a movie or stories you heard growing up influence you. Get those thoughts and pictures out of your head. You are not ruled by demons; They are afraid of you or should be. They are so afraid of you that they will do anything to keep you from learning who you really are. You are royalty, heirs to the Kingdom of God, the child of God himself.

Ephesians 1:19-20   *I also pray that you will understand the incredible greatness of God's power for us who believe him. This is the same mighty power that raised Christ from the dead and seated him in the place of honor at God's right hand in the heavenly realms."*

The enemy comes at us every day. The devil is relentless and merciless. You have to be ready and armed. You are armed and dangerous; you just don't know it. You have been armed and well supplied with everything you need to not only battle but win.

The devil knows this, but you and I forget. We are in the world 24/7, and we give God just one or two hours of our attention each week. It is not enough to drown out the world and all the lies of the enemy. It's not enough to combat the onslaught delivered to our mind and soul each week through television, internet, friends, music, movies, etc.

God has equipped us with powerful tools and weapons. We have his word and his name which gives us the authority we need to trample and tread upon and annihilate the enemy that has already been overpowered and destroyed. As long as we don't know that, the enemy will have his way with us and keep spoon feeding us anxiety, fear, sickness and whatever else we will accept and believe is ours to keep and endure.

Colossians 2:14-15 .....*having canceled the debt ascribed to us in the decrees that stood against us. He took it away, nailing it to the cross! And having disarmed the rulers and authorities, He made a public spectacle of them, triumphing over them by the cross.*

We are either victorious or not. We are either "In Christ" or not. Victory is ours, or it isn't. You and I have to make a decision that the Word of God is true or false and stand on it. When the devil throws sickness and symptoms on you fight back, don't just roll over and play dead. Speak God's word out loud. Reject those symptoms. You can and you will. Reject that runny and itchy nose. Reject that nausea, that diagnosis that is hopeless. You have the greater one living on the inside of you. There is hope. Don't worry or think about all those who died sick. Believe more in God's word than anyone else's circumstances. This is a new day for you, a day to pick up God's word and believe.

Declare this out loud so the Devil can hear you.

I am a child of the most High God.
Jesus is my Lord and savior.
He is my healer and my deliverer.
I can do all things through Christ who paid for all my sins on the cross.
He died for me so I can live and he took with him all my sicknesses and diseases as well.
So I can declare in faith that I am well and these symptoms are lies.
By His Stripes, I am well.
Jesus said I can come to you Father for anything. I am coming to you Father like Jesus taught me in his name. I don't deserve the healing or forgiveness, but I come to you, not for what I deserve

but for what you gave me, mercy and grace. Thank you, Father, for your mercy and grace in my time of need. I am yours.

When those pesky symptoms rise up beat them down.
I resist you, nausea, in the name of Jesus. I am well. I rebuke you and command you off of me. I have been washed by the blood of the Lamb, and I am hidden in him, cleansed and forgiven. I belong to Jesus, and I trust him with my life.

I command my body into obedience to Jesus Christ. My mind, my thoughts, my organs, bones, and systems.

Praise God.

DRIVE THEM OUT

Mark 16:17-18 *These signs will accompany those who believe: in my name they will drive out demons, they will speak new languages. **18** They will pick up serpents [with their hands], and if they drink any deadly thing, it will not harm them. They will lay hands on the sick, and they will recover."*

Signs and wonders will accompany those who believe. Is this you and me? What signs accompany you? Are you driving out demons, speaking in new languages, picking up serpents with your hands? Are you laying hands on the sick? When the disciples could not free the boy with a demon, Jesus rebuked their lack of faith (Luke 9:41). We too need a rebuke from Jesus for our faithlessness. We have a long way to go but don't be disheartened; you are not alone; you are in good company. Most of us do not walk in the authority we have as believers. But that doesn't mean it has to stay that way, or we have to remain that way. There is a whole lot more of the kingdom of God than we are experiencing. Praise God. It just means there is a lot of room for us to grow.

All of these are gifts of the Holy Spirit. We are really hopeless cowards without the power of the Holy Spirit in us. There will be times when we have to come against demons, and when we do, we will be ready because we are full of the Holy Spirit and coming against them with authority.

Cancer is a demon and needs to be driven out. God has given us authority over sickness and evil. The devil won't pack up his bags and leave just because we want him to. We need to drive him out. The devil knows he has to obey the name of Jesus and the power of the Holy Spirit. So we come not in our name but in the name of Jesus which brings power and healing. "It is faith in that name," Peter said to the Jews in the Temple near Solomon's Portico," that this man, whom you see and know, has been made strong. Faith in His name and the faith that comes through it has given this lame man perfect health, in the presence of all of you (ACTS 3: 16).

It is faith in the name of Jesus that gives us authority.

Jesus came to destroy the works of the enemy, and he gave us the same authority. We are God's ambassadors on earth; we represent him. He has given us his name. We are his hands and feet. The same spirit that raised Jesus from the dead lives in us the Bible says in Romans 8:11. This doesn't mean we go around looking for demons, but at the same time, we don't shy away from them either.

The bible says the main offensive weapon against the devil is the word of God. Speak it out loud.

The devil will hear God's word too, and as you begin to believe, the devil will get nervous and try to hold on. But sickness/devil is a liar and has been deceiving you long enough. His time is over, and he must vacate the property. A squatter will squat until the eviction notice comes and is enforced. As long as we are afraid or allow sickness to remain, it's not going to leave. By not driving it out we are giving it permission to stay. It will think it has a right to be there, squatters rights. As long as we are more intimidated by the disease than it is intimidated by us, the disease will remain.

We must drive the spirit of infirmity out. Quit putting up with it. If you had pigs in your kitchen, would you let them stay? Would you put up with them, would you cry and complain and keep cleaning up after them? Would you ask or beg them to leave? No, you would drive them out. The same with sickness and disease. Don't let it stay and overtake you, drive it out! Don't plead and beg, cry and complain. The pigs will just laugh. They aren't going to feel sorry for you and move out. ONLY AUTHORITY and determination will move them.

The longer the pigs or the squatters remain, the deeper the roots. Just because the squatter is unpacked and setting up house, building barns, etc. doesn't mean he is allowed to remain. It's time to evict what doesn't belong. What has moved in and set up shop in your life or home? It's your house. It's your body, and you have been given full authority over your body, your mind, mood, and emotions. You have been given full authority over the devil. Luke 10:19 Behold, I have given you the power 'to tread upon serpents' and scorpions and upon the full force of the enemy and nothing will harm you. He is under your feet.

Psalm 91: 9-11 Because you have the Lord for your refuge
and have made the Most High your stronghold,
[10] No evil shall befall you no affliction come near your tent.
[11] For he commands his angels with regard to you,
to guard you wherever you go

SOMETIMES YOU HAVE TO FIGHT

David could have wished Goliath away or prayed Goliath away. But sometimes you just have to fight Goliath. You can't beg him to go away. You have to exert your authority and command him to leave. It takes guts, knowledge, and understanding and it comes from the Holy Spirit.

I believe we have to fight for our healing. Not that God doesn't fight our battles. He is our defender, our protector, and our ever present help in time of need, the Bible says. God fought and killed Goliath. David says in 1 Samuel chapter 17: verse 37 "The same Lord who delivered me from the claws of the lion and the bear will deliver me from the hand of this Philistine." David knew who his savior was. David knew it was God who would give him the power to overthrow Goliath but he still had to pick up the stones and put them in his sling and throw them at the evil thing advancing against him. He still had to show up. He still had to speak up, and he spoke to Goliath boldly because he had faith and hope and trust that God would back him up. He said, "Today the Lord shall deliver you into my hand....."

> *God is never going to scold you for being to confident in Him. He will never be upset with you for trusting in him too much.*

If you feel sickness coming upon you, fight. Command it to leave you. Jesus told us to "SAY to this mountain "pack up and leave." Do it, say it. Don't worry about what it looks or sounds like. Fight till the end. Don't give up till it's over. What is it going to cost you? You can't pray too much. God is never going to tell you. Why were you so confident in me? He will never be upset with you for trusting in him too much.

I find I have to fight all the time. I have to fight fear and worry by turning to God. It's not like it's a real battle. It is really just putting a stop to emotions or symptoms or fears and worry and remind yourself who you are and who you belong to and what Jesus did for you and gave you. I literally have to remind myself all the time, sometimes multiple times a day who I am and to whom I belong. I remind the cold and flu who they have to bow to. I remind them who God is. He is my Father. I remind God all the time that he gave me through Jesus, and because of Jesus, I have total access to him and freedom from sin. I remind God what Jesus said. I say "Father Jesus said I could come to you and ask you anything." I say "Father I don't deserve your grace and mercy, but I thank you for it." Jesus died and carried my sickness. I thank you, Jesus, for the healing. I say to the sickness. "By his stripes, I am healed." I say to the symptoms, fever "I rebuke you and command you to leave me." Don't quit, don't give up till Goliath is dead.

At the end of this book are many declarations. These are how you fight. These are just starter declarations. You will eventually write your own, and you too will triumph like David did against Goliath.

ASK

James 4:2 *You do not possess because you do not ask.*

The Bible it tells us over and over and over again to ASK.
Bring your concerns and burdens to God. ASK and let God take
it from there. Yet for some reason when we are faced with a
trial, a sick child, a boss who is impossible to work with or a
failing marriage we try to go it alone. We may talk to our family
and friends, read the latest books, or go for counseling, but If we
don't take it to God, then we don't give God the opportunity to
answer our prayers. We do not have because we do not ask!
That's right; we have not because we ask not!

I say ask God for everything—to take your headache away, for a
good parking spot, to help your child ace the TAKS test, the
raise you've been waiting for, etc., etc., etc., And be very
specific in your prayer request so that you will truly KNOW that
it's GOD who is answering. For example, don't just pray for
marriages in general. Pray for your marriage and any marriage
you know of that needs prayer, but specifically, name them and
their needs.

Years ago I heard a CEO comment on what surprised her most
about her job. She said it was when she gave her employees
their reviews she would ask them what they wanted for a raise
and 9/10 times they would ask for less than she was willing to
give them! Wow, if they had only known. So in life, I say, pray
and ask big. Think about it...when we find out someone is sick
what do we typically pray for? So often we pray for the person
to have the strength to endure the illness, for patience, for their
family . We don't ask for healing—we don't go for the miracle!
The general thinking is if the person is sick then God's will must
be for the person to be ill and we certainly don't want to go
against God's will. But just as scripture says, we are called to
ASK. To the person who say *"what if it's not God's will to heal
the person?"* I say, *"what if it is? What if God is just waiting*

for someone to ask Him?" God is a gentleman. So when people ask me to pray for them and they are sick I always ask for complete healing. If it's a situation that the doctor's say the person can't be healed I think, OK it's going to be easier for God to get the glory on this one when the person is healed. There was a lady in my Bible study group whose son's eardrum shattered and the doctor said he'll never hear out of that ear again. But we didn't stop praying for him after that diagnosis. And you know what, his hearing has slightly started to return, praise be to God, and we are continuing to pray for complete restoration of that ear!

My Bible lists Jesus' miracles in chronological order—of the 35 miracles, 27 were regarding HEALING. When Jesus was here on Earth people constantly came to Him for healing and He never once turned anyone away. Think about that—He healed everyone who asked. And I believe He will do the same for us today. In Pope Benedict XVI new book Jesus of Nazareth, he says of Jesus "He does not come bearing the sword of the revolutionary. He comes with the gift of healing. Healing our bodies, souls, spirits, our marriages, families, friendships, neighbors, countries and yes our world."

I did a quick Google search on where in the Bible it says for us to ASK. The result was three pages long, but I wanted to share with you a few of my favorite scripture verses where it says to ASK.

Luke 11:9 and 10 *And I tell you, ask and you will receive; seek and you will find; knock and the door will be opened to you. For every one who asks, receives; and the one who seeks, finds; and to the one who knocks, the door will be opened.*

1 Kings 3:5 *In Gibeon the Lord appeared to Solomon in a dream at night. God said, Ask something of me and I will give to you.*

Matthew 21:22 *Whatever you ask for in prayer with faith, you will receive.*

John 14:13-14 *And whatever you ask in my name, I will do it, so that theFather may be glorified in the son. If you ask anything of me in my name, I will do it.*

John 15:7 *If you remain in me and my words remain in you, ask for whatever you want and it will be done for you.*

James 4:2b *You do not possess because you do not ask.*

John 16:23 and 24 *On that day you will not question me about anything. Amen, amen I say to you, whatever you ask the Father in my name He will give you. Until now you have not asked anything in my name; ask and you will receive, so that your joy may be complete.*

James 1:5 and 6 *But if any of you lacks wisdom, he should ASK God who gives to all generously and ungrudgingly, and he will be given it. But he should ask in faith, not doubting, for the one who doubts is like a wave of the sea that is driven and tossed about by the wind.*

We don't like asking. We think for some reason we are bothering God. Why is asking so important? When we ask for something from God and He gives it to us or He does it, we can tell everyone all about it. Then God gets all the glory.

AUTHOR Pam Criss

TEN LEPERS

Luke 17:15-16 *And one of them, realizing he had been healed, returned, glorifying God in a loud voice; ¹⁶ and he fell at the feet of Jesus and thanked him.*

This is the story of one the ten lepers Jesus healed. The ten lepers saw Jesus and asked him to have pity on them. Jesus told them to show themselves to the priests. The priests determined whether or not a person was clean or unclean. To be a leper was to be unclean and they were put out of the community and labeled guilty (see Leviticus 5:3). An unclean person could not live, let alone worship, with the rest of his family and friends. If they were diagnosed clean, they could return to the community, to worship and to their old lives. Leviticus explains what happens to a person diagnosed with leprosy in the Israel of the Old Testament.

> **Leviticus13:45-46** *"The leprous person who has the disease shall wear torn clothes and let the hair of his head hang loose, and he shall cover his upper lip and cry out, 'Unclean, unclean.' ⁴⁶ He shall remain unclean as long as he has the disease. He is unclean. He shall live alone. His dwelling shall be outside the camp.*

Ten were healed, but only one came back to thank Jesus and give glory and praise to God. He was a foreigner or Gentile, and upon noticing, he was healed of leprosy, turned back to find and thank Jesus. He gave the first fruits of his healing to God. The bible says with a loud voice he glorified God. I wonder what that sounded like. Did he jump up and down and shout "Thank you God; thank you, Father, You are my Lord and King, you are the great I Am"? Did he look up to heaven with hands raised and cry out "thank you, Father, I praise your name and believe in you and worship you?" Did he run around telling everyone "God saved me! He healed me?" I can imagine him crying with great joy.

He then gave homage to Jesus by falling at his feet. He worshiped Jesus because he knew he was from God. Falling prostrate before God is an outward sign of the condition of a person's heart. He publicly demonstrated his submission to God. He chose to give the God of Israel the praise and honor and glory he deserved, and he did it immediately. He went to God first, before the priest and even before his family.

Always thank God first even before you start spreading the good news. Let God be the first to hear the good news from your very own lips.

- **Additional Reading:** Luke 17:11-19, 1 Chronicles 29:20, Rev. 7:11

NIP IT IN THE BUD

Whether it's sin or sickness, it is important to "nip it in the bud." The minute you recognize sickness or fear trying to get a grip on you, resist it immediately. Do not let it get a foothold and talk you into believing it has power over you. Do not let sickness have an inch or it will take a mile

Ephesians 4:27 *and do not leave room for the devil.*

I can't stress this enough. It is vital that you attack the virus, infection or disease immediately at the first sign or symptom. Attack it with your faith and the knowledge that you have been healed and forgiven and delivered from all sickness, and fear and worry. If you don't fight with faith immediately, doubt will creep in, and sickness has a foothold. We aren't faithless. We all believe in something. Let's not put our faith in sickness. Let's not believe in its power and let it have dominion over us.

Once you entertain sickness or disease, it's hold will grow stronger. It thrives on doubt and fear. Do not feed it or give it ammunition or fuel. The longer you entertain the symptoms and allow them space; they will set up shop, dig in their heals and remain as long as they are tolerated. Chop off the head of doubt and the sooner, the better.

Many days I will wake up feeling sick or nervous, and my mind will start to imagine sickness, and start to fear. This is when we must make a decision to put our thoughts on Christ. Start speaking to yourself at once. Start to remind yourself who you are and to whom you belong. Start to tell God you love him and trust him. I do this immediately, at the first sign of trouble.

I say...

" I trust you, Lord."
"You are my ever-present help in time of need."
"I believe in you, and I am healed."
"By His stripes, I am healed."
"Jesus has healed me, and I am healed."
"Jesus took my sins and my diseases to the cross with him, and I am free from sickness." "Jesus loves me, and I am his."
"He is my defender, my strength, and my champion."
"I will never fear."
"He takes care of me...."

Recognize those sick and fearful thoughts for what they are, a manipulation of the devil. Tools of his trade to hook you and conquer you.

HUNGRY FOR THE SPIRIT

Matthew 5:6 *"Blest are they who hunger and thirst for holiness; they shall have their fill."*

Hungry? But just ate? Then maybe what we are hungry for is not food. Maybe it is for the Lord. Our souls will not be satisfied until we sup with the Lord. How can we have supper with the Lord? Revelation 3:30 says "here I stand, knocking at the door, I will enter his house and have supper with him, and he with me." And, that is a two way door. Mathew 7:7 says "Knock and it will be opened to you." So, knock on His door, invite Him to enter your home, your life, your heart, and have dinner with you. Set a place at your table for Him. Have common conversation with Him. Set aside some time for Him. Put Him on your calendar.

Hungry? Jesus speaks about including the poor in His parable in Luke 14:12-14. Notice Jesus does not correct the man who in Luke 14:14 says, "Happy is he who eats bread in the kingdom of God." (Seems only to be thinking of his belly.) Instead, Jesus expounds on the food idea with the parable of a large dinner. The invited all have excuses, so instructions are given to go out into the streets and alleys and bring in the poor and the crippled, the blind and the lame."

The choice is yours. Will you be the one with an excuse? Will you be one of the poor, the crippled, the blind or the lame? How hungry are you? Jesus is the bread of life, the sustenance of life. How do I get an audience with Him? How do I get His attention?

How do I get His attention as did blind Bartimaeus?
How do I touch Him as did the lady with the issue of blood?
How are my eyes to be opened as were the men on the road to Emmaus? How can I place my fingers into his side as Thomas did?

If you are hungry for Him, it is He who is initiating the encounter. It is He who is knocking on your door. It is His power drawing you. Will you open your door? How far will you open your door? Will you just barely crack it open to let Him peek at you? Or are you willing and ready to open it wide?

Afraid? Ask: Why am I afraid? What will he ask me to do?""What will I have to give up?" What will others think of me? We worry because we fail to know His love for us. He will never leave us or forsake us. He will never ask us to do anything beyond our capabilities. (Have never know Him to ask anyone to give up anything. It is His love that will trump anything that is bad for us.) Will he stretch us? Yes! Will He ask us to trust Him? Yes! Will He ask us to take a step in faith? Yes!

He knows us better than we know ourselves. He knows our gifts and talents. He knows the desires of our hearts. It is He who made us. He who gifted us. It is He who puts the desires on our hearts. He too will make us come to Him. He will nourish us. He will give us growth. He will make us bloom. He gives all the courage, strength, knowledge, wisdom, understanding that we need.

Read and meditate on Mark 10:46-52; Luke 42b-48; Luke 24:13-31; John 20:24-29

AUTHOR Sheila Lovelace

POWER IN THE NAME OF JESUS

John 14:12-14 *Very truly I tell you, whoever believes in me will do the works I have been doing, and they will do even greater things than these, because I am going to the Father.* *13 And I will do whatever you ask in my name, so that the Father may be glorified in the Son.* *14 You may ask me for anything in my name, and I will do it.*

Jesus told us over and over again to ask him for anything. This is how he brings his father glory (John 14:12-14). Every time he tells us to ask the Father in his name, he follows it up with a promise that we will receive whatever we ask for when we come to him in faith and in love, no if and's or buts about it.

Matthew 7:7 *"Ask and it will be given to you; seek and you will find; knock and the door will be opened to you. 8 For everyone who asks receives;"*

Jesus promises that if you ask, you will receive. That is a promise. God cannot resist us when we come in Jesus's name. The Father will do anything for Jesus. That is why Jesus gave us his name and told us to use it. We come believing we are good enough to ask because when we come in Jesus' name, we are telling God, we believe Jesus has forgiven us all our sins and made us worthy (good enough) to ask. God can not be separated from his name. His power and authority are attached to his name. His name gives us authority and is recognized here on earth, in heaven, and under the earth. All evil must bow to the name of Jesus.

Jesus has given us not only his name but the authority that goes with it. Just like the American Ambassador to Great Brittain represents the President of the United States of America and has the authority to do so, we represent Jesus on the earth through the church. The Ambassador to a foreign country speaks in the name of the president. The police officer comes in the name of the law to arrest someone. That officer has the power, the law of the city or county he represents gives him or her. We obey traffic officers because they represent the law, not because they are big and tough. We too are ambassadors, ambassadors of Christ and we represent Him on earth. We have that privilege and the power that goes with it when we remain in Him and connected to the church, the body of Christ.

In the Old Testament, God's name was so honored that it was not spoken or even written by anyone ever, even in the Torah. They used letters without vowels so the people would not use his name by accident. That is how much respect they had for God's name. Today he has given us his name and all the authority and power that comes with his name because we are one with him and the Holy Spirit lives in us.

Smith Wigglesworth, a Christian evangelist from the United Kingdom who died in 1947, wrote a book called "Ever Increasing Faith" where he describes what happened in Wales when he was asked to pray for a man named Lazarus. Lazarus worked in the tin mines and became sick with Tuberculosis. He was bed ridden for six years and on the verge of death when Wigglesworth brought seven men with him to pray for him. They gathered around his bed and all held hands in a circle.

> "Then Wigglesworth said, "We are not going to pray; we are just going to use the Name of Jesus." They all knelt and whispered that one word, "Jesus! Jesus! Jesus! The power of God fell, and then it lifted. Five times it fell and lifted, as the little group spoke that magnificent Name. The man in the bed was unmoved. The sixth time the power of God came down on that man, it remained. "The power of God is here," Wigglesworth told him. "It is yours to accept." The man's lips began to move. He made a confession. He said, "I have been bitter in my heart, and I know I have grieved the Spirit of God. I am helpless. I cannot lift my hands, nor even lift a spoon to my mouth." Wigglesworth said, "Repent, and God will hear you." He repented and cried out, "Oh God, let this be to Thy glory." When he said that, the power of God went through

him. Wigglesworth said, "As we again said, 'Jesus! Jesus! Jesus!' the bed shook, and the man shook....I sat and watched that man get up and dress. We sang the doxology as he walked down the steps."

Phil 2:10 *so that at the name of Jesus EVERY KNEE WILL BOW, of those who are in heaven and on earth and under the earth.*

Peter says to the crowd in Acts 3:16 right after the lame man was healed, *"Through faith in the name of Jesus, this man was healed —and you know how crippled he was before. Faith in Jesus' name has healed him before your very eyes."* There is power when we mix faith with the name of Jesus.

When we have faith in the name of Jesus we don't hope we get well, we know. When we have faith, we rest in him. Faith is peace and hope and rest, no longer striving, stressing or wishing. God cannot ignore us when we trust in his name. He loves us so much he gave us his name.

GOD HEALS NOW - TODAY - STILL!

John 14:13-14 *And whatever you ask in my name, I will do, so that the Father may be glorified in the Son. If you ask anything of me in my name, I will do it.*

This scripture speaks volumes. Not only does Jesus want to give his father all the glory but it shows us how God is still healing today. Jesus said "You will do even greater things because I am going to the father (I am going to heaven). He is talking about us now!!!! He is in heaven and expecting us now, to do greater things. Healing is supposed to happen now, today, while Jesus is in heaven, not just when Jesus walked on earth. Jesus didn't say we would do greater works then he did if healing wasn't ours still today.

MYTHS REGARDING HEALING

MYTH NUMBER 1 - Healing depends on us. We have to earn it or do something to deserve it.   If it depends on us, we will never get healed. We can never earn it. No one ever has or ever will or ever could.

It doesn't depend on us. Jesus healed everyone. EVERYONE! The good and the bad, the poor and the rich. When Jesus healed the multitudes that came to him, he didn't evaluate them he just healed them. If we think for one minute that our healing is based on our sinless condition than we will never be healed because we will always fall short. We have fallen short.

God heals everyone. He doesn't pick and choose. Either God heals everyone or no one. If he chooses who to heal and who not to heal, then we will always be the ones (in our own eyes) on the "not to list". We will always be the one he chooses not to heal. We will always put ourselves in that category. We would never have faith because we would always question whether or not we are the ones he WILL NOT HEAL. If we believe that there are some that don't get healed, it will always be us. We will never have the faith of the Canaanite woman who knew she didn't deserve it but went for the mercy and grace of God anyway. She would not take no for an answer because she knew God's nature and that he couldn't resist her faith and hope and trust in him.

I don't trust in my sinlessness or goodness to earn me a place in heaven or healing or God's favor, but I know that through Christ's mercy and grace, healing and forgiveness and favor are mine. I am his favored daughter, not because of me but because of Jesus Christ. My faith is in him and his goodness, mercy, and grace and the good things he has done rather than on me and my own. My confidence comes from him. It is him I trust.

I met a woman once whose grandmother died of Alzheimer's and her mother died of Alzheimer's. She decided it is her fate as well. She has a choice though to believe it is God's will to heal her or not. Faith is not believing God can, but believing God will. This is so important. We all know God can just say the word. What we don't believe and know apparently is that he has already spoken the word. Jesus is the word of God himself. He chose to offer himself up for us. MAKE A STAND. DRAW A LINE IN THE SAND. STAND FIRM knowing if you don't you are passing on the same legacy to your daughter and her daughters. Are you willing to have faith to believe and ask in faith for the healing that he wants for you? God does not receive glory in your sickness. He does, however, receive glory when you get healed.

MYTH Number 2 - God uses sickness to teach us a lesson. Are you a Mother or Father? Have you or would you ever put sickness on a child to teach him a lesson? If you believe that God is teaching you a lesson, by all means, learn the lesson and get on with your life. If sickness is the only way to reach you, sickness may be what God uses to rescue or save you.

John 9:2-3 *"Rabbi," his disciples asked him, "why was this man born blind? Was it because of his own sins or his parents' sins? It was not because of his sins or his parents' sins," Jesus answered. "This happened so the power of God could be seen in him."*
Just maybe you are going through something to bring God glory. Imagine the glory God will receive when you become well. Will God get the Glory. Will you tell others about what God did for you? Usually, we hear about some new treatment or medicine or therapy very rarely do we hear that God healed someone. I always marveled at the 10 lepers. Why did only one come back to thank God? I know why. I see it all the time. The others had someone or something else to thank. It was that medicine that finally kicked in..

No wonder God never gets the glory. They say in Africa people are healed in churches all the time. They have no hospitals like we do. They have no medicine like we do. They have to trust God.

In Acts chapter three we hear about when Peter and John went to pray and the met the lame man on the way to the temple. Peter said to the man. "Silver and Gold I do not have but what I do have I give you. "In the name of Jesus Christ of Nazareth Rise up and walk." They had no medicine, no hospital to offer; they had something better. Peter said I don't have what you are looking for, but I have something better. I don't have money, but I do have healing.

You may be going through something but be of good cheer. Keep trusting Jesus like the woman with the issue of blood who left her home knowing if she just touched his cloak she would get well, or the Centurion that told Jesus "if you just say the word I know my servant will be well" or the Canaanite woman who wouldn't take no for an answer till Jesus healed her daughter. Keep trusting like the FOUR men who carried their friend to Jesus on a stretcher. They dug through a roof because they knew, without a doubt, Jesus wouldn't let them down.

MYTH Number 3 - But don't I need to suffer and offer it up.

I hear this all the time. Most of us were raised with the notion that we need just to offer it up. Yes, this is true. Offer it up. Offer up your complaining, your whining, you fear and worry. Offer up to God your faith and trust in him. Offer to God your suffering as you love those who are unlovable. Offer that suffering up to God. We have many opportunities to offer up to God our suffering and it's not sickness. Offer up to God your feelings of rejection as you tell others about Jesus. Offer up your time and money for the sake of helping others. There are many ways we can suffer. God calls us to suffer for his name sake, not for the sake of suffering.

MYTH Number 4 – If you ask and God doesn't answer right away it must not be his will to heal you. Sometimes God is stretching our faith and teaching us to persevere or how to fight and stand for what is ours. IF it doesn't happen today, wait till tomorrow or the next day or the next. Rest in him and trust it is coming.

Sometimes we fight against our own healing by complaining or speaking as if we never prayed at all. We say things like, "I will never get well" or we say "I am dying" right after we asked God to heal us. We say "I have Cancer," "I am so sick," or we tell our family and friends how bad it is and describe our symptoms. Instead, let's speak like a man or woman of faith who says "I am healed," I do not have cancer because cancer is under my feet and God has healed me." "By his stripes, I am healed," I am alive and well, and God is my healer and deliverer and has set me free," "I am getting better every day", I will live and declare the works of the Lord."

WHAT COMPLAINING GETS YOU!!

Numbers 14:2-3 *² All the Israelites grumbled against Moses and Aaron, the whole community saying to them, "If only we had died in the land of Egypt," or "If only we would die here in the wilderness! ³ Why is the Lord bringing us into this land only to have us fall by the sword? Our wives and little ones will be taken as spoil. Would it not be better for us to return to Egypt?"*

The Israelites grumbled and complained one too many times. They had seen the goodness of the Lord yet doubted. They had seen the Lord open up the Red Sea allowing them to walk through on dry ground, yet they couldn't believe God would take care of them. They walked in the midst of the sea the bible says. They walked between two walls of water. It was phenomenal what they experienced. Pharaoh and his army were coming against them only to run up against the God in a cloud while the Israelites walked into the sea.

Only a short journey into the wilderness and already they forgot their Lord. The Lord was with them proving his goodness over and over, and all they could do was complain and shrink back in fear when their faith was tested. They preferred the shackles to freedom with God. They preferred to die than believe God could do what he said he could do and give them what he promised to give them, THE PROMISED LAND. This is the land God promised them when he rescued them from Egypt. The land was indeed flowing with milk and honey, but all they saw were the "giants" living there. 12 people were sent to investigate the land, and ten came back complaining. "We were like grasshoppers," the men said upon returning. "They are too strong for us" Read the whole account in Numbers 13 and 14, it is a great story.

Don't be the dog crouching in the back of the cage remaining in fear of freedom and the unknown. Don't hold onto the familiar when you can walk into victory in the presence and protection of the one who loves you unconditionally. If God is leading you to forgive, he will be there with you the whole way. Don't be like Israelites and prefer to remain comfortable and miss all that God has for you. God is calling you to love your mother, brother, husband, son, daughter that is hard to love. If you are following and trusting God, he is leading and where he leads is wonderful. It may not be easy, love and forgiveness are not easy but when you die to yourself, resurrection comes, and it comes quickly. No one can even comprehend what the Lord has in store for those who love him and go where he leads.

Don't be sidetracked by thoughts and feelings. They will keep you from receiving your promised land. The Israelites preferred captivity to the land flowing with milk and honey that the Lord promised them and proved it with their mouths. They not only complained, they spoke like they knew what would happen. They saw themselves as victims instead of conquerors. God has made us conquerors, not victims.

They complained. They may as well have said. God we don't believe you or trust you or want to continue following you. We prefer to remain as slaves, and we want our children and their children also to remain as slaves. We would rather do it our way and live and rule our own lives. God gave them what they wanted, what they spoke of. They remained 40 years in the desert until each one died. Their children had to endure 40 years in the desert.

What words come out of your mouth, words of faith or doubt and fear? What is your legacy going to be? What are you speaking over your life? Who do you want to run your life? Who are you following, trusting? What do you want to leave your children? Israel received exactly what they spoke and believed they would receive. Be careful about what you say, you may just receive it. If you say "Bad things always happen to us" Then chances are bad things will always happen to you. If you say, "all of my family gets cancer than chances are so will you."

The Israelites saw themselves as conquered. Therefore they couldn't believe anything else. They saw the enemy as bigger than God. They called themselves grasshoppers because that is what they felt like and believed about themselves. They believed they were like grasshoppers about to be squashed. They had no faith in God or his power to rescue or protect them.

GOD IS JUST AND MERCIFUL

Numbers 12:9-10 *⁹ The anger of the Lord burned against them, and he left them.¹⁰ When the cloud lifted from above the tent, Miriam's skin was leprous.*

We have a sinful nature. Miriam was jealous of her brother Moses and collaborated with Aaron and complained about Moses and his leadership. The Lord heard and punished Miriam. When Miriam complained against Moses, she was coming against God. Moses was God's choice, God's anointed. Miriam became a leper.

We are all doomed to sin and the consequences of our sins. OR ARE WE? Today when a man murders someone and then has remorse, it's not acceptable to let him go just because he is sorry. We demand Justice, and so does God. God is a just God. When we sin, someone has to pay the price. There is a cost associated with every sin. We can't just be sorry and get out of the consequence or can we? How can we?

Exodus 21:23-24 But if there is any further injury, then you shall appoint as a penalty life for life, eye for eye, tooth for tooth, hand for hand, foot for foot, burn for burn, wound for wound, bruise for bruise.

Sin kills. Sin kills our relationship with God. There is a punishment associated with sin and the punishment is ultimately death. Our relationship with God dies. We die a spiritual death.

Proverbs 11:19 Truly the righteous attain life,
but whoever pursues evil finds death.

God is both just and merciful, so he worked our salvation out for us. Our salvation from death AND the punishment of sin. God sent his son to earth to take the punishment we deserved. Jesus obeyed the Father, the Bible says even unto death, death on a cross. Jesus paid the punishment for all sin, the sin of the whole world. We no longer have to pay the price of our sin. God did it for us because, throughout the ages, we have proven over and over again that we cannot get it right. We cannot be righteous and sinless. We cannot obey God on our own. Jesus came and did it for us. He was the only one who could. We could not save ourselves. We needed a savior.

If we believe we are forgiven but yet still must bear the burden or the consequences of our sin then .... We would all be like Miriam running around with leprosy, in order to pay for our crimes. *For the Law was given through Moses; grace and truth came through Jesus Christ* (John 1:17). The law says "an eye for an eye," Jesus came to bring us grace and mercy. We are not able to bear the burden of our sin, and neither are we able to bear the burden of our punishment or the consequences of sin. Sin is death, spiritual death, eternal death and separation from God. Thankfully God knew that and decided, while he still had to be just, he could, in fact, take the punishment for us and that is what he did. We all deserve death but thanks be to God, we have forgiveness instead through the death of Jesus Christ, our savior.

Miriam received the punishment of leprosy, but Moses interceded for her and asked for healing. Moses was the mediator between God and man. Today it is Jesus. Jesus is our intercessor, our mediator. He goes before God reminding God of the blood he shed for us when the accuser rises up against us.

God does not hold our sins against us. He can't. He held them against Jesus. Either Jesus took your sins and mine or he didn't. The bible says the sins of your past, present and future are all gone. The sin you haven't committed yet is really already forgiven. There is no sin counted against you except the sin you choose to keep.

God wants us to know how hideous sin is. Our sins cost Jesus his life. Our sins weighed on him heavily. Since we know what sin cost Jesus, cost our father, we stay away from it. It is repugnant to us. I personally do not want to be out of fellowship with God for even a second, so I am on the look out how to avoid sin.

When my husband gets sick, I would sometimes hear myself say "Just get up. You are fine." The next day I am down with the same illness. It's not that God is inflicting me. I don't believe God puts sickness on anyone ever, but I opened the door to evil and when I did, sickness came in. God uses everything to mold us and grow us. He turns everything to good for us.

Sin brings us out of fellowship with God. We just need to repent and walk back in. The longer you are out the harder it is to get back in. Don't waste a minute being out of touch with God. The reason it takes you so long to get back to God is your own distractions and beliefs and habits. The longer we are away and in sin the more distractions keep us away and have a strong hold on us.

Don't wait till you get leprosy to look for God. Spend time with God, so he can shape you and mold you and grow you up in the Holy Spirit.

THE WORD OF GOD IS MEDICINE

Deuteronomy 30:19 *I call heaven and earth as witnesses today against you, that I have set before you life and death, blessing and cursing; therefore choose life, that both you and your descendants may live;*

Sicknesses and diseases attack. The flu, for example, invades your body and attaches to your cells and then multiplies. That is what they do, that is how the virus works. You can get the flu just by being around someone with the flu. Sickness travels and is caught.

Jesus came to bring us health and life and not just any old miserable life but abundant life. He gave it to us, but we have to go get it, receive it and know that it is ours. There are times when we simply ask God to heal us, and it is done. We receive it immediately, and all we have to do is ask. Sometimes we have to actually fight for it because we have an enemy that comes to kill, steal and destroy our health. (John 10:10)

God's word is medicine not just for our soul but for our bodies as well. Medicine will not do us any good until we actually consume it. The same is true with the word of God. The word of God is more powerful than any medicine. The Bible says this about the power of God's word to heal us.

Proverbs 4:20-22 My son, pay attention to what I say;
turn your ear to my words.
21 Do not let them out of your sight,
keep them within your heart;
22 for they are life to those who find them
and health to one's whole body.

Psalm 107:20 He sent forth his word to heal them,
and snatched them from the grave.

We have to open the word of God and read it and read it daily. We have to choose life and sometimes that choice requires us to do something.

"For it is the Lord, your God, who goes with you to fight for you against your enemies and give you victory." **Deuteronomy 20:4**

Take hold of what God has given you and promises you. Declare the word of God and what is yours. The word of God is the Sword of the Spirit, a weapon used to battle evil (Ephesians 6:17). I have attached a short list of Healing Scriptures to read. See the back of the book for the full list or go to my website to download. www.where2ormoregather.com/documents/

Isaiah 53:5 But he was pierced for our sins, crushed for our iniquity. He bore the punishment that makes us whole, by **his** wounds we were healed.

Psalm 103:1-4, 11-12 Let all that I am praise the Lord; with my whole heart, I will praise his holy name. Let all that I am praise the Lord; may I never forget the good things he does for me. He forgives all my sins and heals all my diseases. He redeems me from death and crowns me with love and tender mercies. …. For as high as the heavens are above the earth, so great is his love for those who fear him; as far as the east is from the west so far has he removed our transgressions from us.

Mark 11:22-25 "Have faith in God," Jesus answered. "Truly I tell you, if anyone says to this mountain, 'Go, throw yourself into the sea,' and does not doubt in their heart but believes that what they say will happen, it will be done for them. Therefore I tell you, whatever you ask for in prayer, believe that you have received it, and it will be yours. And when you stand praying, if you hold anything against anyone, forgive them, so that your Father in heaven may forgive you your sins."

John 14:11-14 Believe me when I say that I am in the Father and the Father is in me; or at least believe on the evidence of the works themselves. Very truly I tell you, whoever believes in me will do the works I have been doing, and they will do even greater things than these, because I am going to the Father. And I will do whatever you ask in my name, so that the Father may be glorified in the Son. You may ask me for anything in my name, and I will do it.

Psalm 30:2 Lord my God, I called to you for help, and you healed me.

Psalm 41:3 The Lord sustains them on their sickbed and restores them from their bed of illness.

Psalm 91 Those who live in the shelter of the Most High will find rest in the shadow of the Almighty. This I declare about the Lord: He alone is my refuge, my place of safety; he is my God, and I trust him. For he will rescue you from every trap and protect you from deadly disease. He will cover you with his feathers. He will shelter you with his wings. His faithful promises are your armor and protection. Do not be afraid of the terrors of the night, nor the arrow that flies in the day. Do not dread the disease that stalks in darkness, nor the disaster that strikes at midday. Though a thousand fall at your side, though ten thousand are dying around you, these evils will not touch you. Just open your eyes, and see how the wicked are punished. If you make the Lord your refuge, if you make the Most High your shelter, no evil will conquer you; no plague will come near your home. For he will order his angels to protect you wherever you go. They will hold you up with their hands so you won't even hurt your foot on a stone. You will trample upon lions and cobras; you will crush fierce lions and serpents under your feet! The Lord says, "I will rescue those who love me. I will protect those who trust in my name. When they call on me, I will answer; I will be with them in trouble. I will rescue and honor them. I will reward them with a long life and give them my salvation."

Matthew   15:29-31 Jesus left there and went along the Sea of Galilee. Then he went up on a mountainside and sat down. **30** Great crowds came to him, bringing the lame, the blind, the crippled, the mute and many others, and laid them at his feet; and he healed them. **31** The people were amazed when they saw the mute speaking, the crippled made well, the lame walking and the blind seeing. And they praised the God of Israel.

Romans   8:32 He who did not spare his own Son but handed him over for us all, how will he not also give us everything else along with him?

2 Corinthians 4:18 So we fix our eyes not on what is seen, but on what is unseen, since what is seen is temporary, but what is unseen is eternal.

YOU HAVE THE SAME SPIRIT DAVID HAD
- David <u>Part 1</u>

1 Samuel 17:8-11 *"He stood and shouted to the ranks of Israel: "Why come out in battle formation? I am a Philistine, and you are Saul's servants. Choose one of your men, and have him come down to me. If he beats me in combat and kills me, we will be your vassals; but if I beat him and kill him, you shall be our vassals and serve us." The Philistine continued: "I defy the ranks of Israel today. Give me a man and let us fight together." When Saul and all Israel heard this challenge of the Philistine, they were stunned and terrified.*

This may be the most famous battle scene ever recorded. The entire army, including King Saul, was terrified of the Philistines because of Goliath, their champion. For 40 days and nights, the bible says, Goliath came forward and challenged the Israelites. Every day Goliath came forward and took his stand insulting the army of Israel and making the challenge and every day Israel shrank back in terror. No one wanted to take on Goliath. No one wanted to risk the entire nation. No one trusted God to help them or save the nation.

Goliath was six cubits and a span or somewhere between 7 and 9 feet tall depending on the size of cubit which is the length of the forearm. The cubit is measured from the elbow to the tip of the middle finger (approximately 18 inches) which would make Goliath 9 feet tall assuming the forearm of a man has always been 18 inches.

David, a young boy, saved a nation by offering to take on Goliath one on one. David is asked by his father Jesse to bring supplies to his older brothers who are on the battle lines in formation facing the Philistines.

When David hears the Philistine and sees the army shrink back in fear, he is amazed and says who is this....*" uncircumcised Philistine that he should insult the armies of the living God?"*

David says *"I will fight him. Have no fear; I will go."* He told the king that he would take care of the Philistine like he took care of the bear and the lion that attacked his sheep.

"Your servant used to tend his father's sheep, and whenever a lion or bear came to carry off a sheep from the flock, I would chase after it, attack it, and snatch the prey from its mouth. If it attacked me, I would seize it by the throat, strike it, and kill it. Your servant has killed both a lion and a bear. This uncircumcised Philistine will be as one of them, because he has insulted the armies of the living God." David continued: "The same Lord who delivered me from the claws of the lion and the bear will deliver me from the hand of this Philistine" **(1 Samuel 17:34-37).**

King Saul said to David "Go, and the Lord be with you!"

So David, unable to walk in the king's armor went without taking with him to meet Goliath, only a sling and five stones he found in the river.

What guts. How confident he was in his God. His confidence came from spending time with God and experiencing his mighty hand and saving power. Spend time in his presence and watch what God will do with you and to you and for you. You will be like David. You too have the same Holy Spirit living inside of you. David had the Holy Spirit on him. Take time to read the entire story of David and Goliath found in 1 Samuel chapter 17. Read chapter 16 also. We read about how Samuel the prophet anointed David

"The Lord said: There—anoint him, for this is the one! Then Samuel, with the horn of oil in hand, anointed him in the midst of his brothers, and from that day on, the spirit of the Lord rushed upon David
(1 Samuel 16 verses 12-13)."

Before Pentecost, before Jesus ascended into heaven the Holy Spirit would come on only certain individuals called by God to be prophets/kings/priests. That is why Jesus said, you have to let me go.

John 16:7 *"But I tell you the truth, it is better for you that I go. For if I do not go, the Advocate (Holy Spirit) will not come to you. But if I go, I will send him to you."*

And that is just what happened at Pentecost. Jesus sent the Holy Spirit to the disciples in the upper room where Jesus told them to wait. Jesus sent the Holy Spirit to the church so we could do what God calls us to do, love who God calls us to love and go where God calls us to go and be the men and women of God he calls us to be. We can't do it without the power of the Holy Spirit.

You and I now have the Holy Spirit within us because we have chosen Christ. We all go through the sacraments, Baptism, Penance, First Communion, and Confirmation. Just as we have to one day take Jesus for ourselves, the same is true for the Holy Spirit. We have to renew our Confirmation and receive the fullness of the Holy Spirit. We all receive him when we receive Jesus. But we won't walk in the power until we invite the Holy Spirit into our lives. Jesus says in:

Luke 11:13 *"If you then, who are wicked, know how to give good gifts to your children, how much more will the Father in heaven give the holy Spirit to those who ask him?"*

Do you want to walk in the Power of the Holy Spirit like David did, you can too? It's up to you. David was fearless because he was walking in the power of the Holy Spirit. David was so full of God that he couldn't help but be confident and bold. He talked like this because he was certain. He was sure God was with him. How sure are you?

THE VOICE OF THE GIANT - David
Part 2

1 Samuel 17:45-47 *Then David said to the Philistine, "You come to me with a sword, with a spear, and with a javelin. But I come to you in the name of the Lord of hosts, the God of the armies of Israel, whom you have defied. This day the Lord will deliver you into my hand, and I will strike you and take your head from you. And this day I will give the carcasses of the camp of the Philistines to the birds of the air and the wild beasts of the earth, that all the earth may know that there is a God in Israel. Then all this assembly shall know that the Lord does not save with sword and spear; for the battle is the Lord's, and He will give you into our hands."*

When Goliath saw David, he said to him. "What am I a dog that you come at me with sticks?" and the Philistine cursed David by his gods and continued saying "Come to me, and I will give your flesh to the birds of the air and the beasts of the field!" David was unmoved by the voice of the giant. The giant did not scare him though he threatened.

We have to be like David with the voices in our head that move us to react in anger, fear or worry. We scare at first sight of danger. One bad report and fear takes the place of our faith. We are easily angered or offended, and we react without thinking with anger, rage, and get defensive and fight back. David was undaunted. He didn't let the words of Goliath penetrate he had his shield of faith up. Those fiery darts were quenched and could do no damage. David wasn't going to let an uncircumcised enemy rule him.

David fought the Philistine. Who did David think he was? Where did he get the nerve to speak so boldly? How did he know for sure God would be with him? We learned from chapter 16 that David was no ordinary young man. He was anointed with the power of the Holy Spirit.

David knew who he was, and he knew who Goliath wasn't. David knew he belonged to God and he also knew that Goliath did not belong to God. The same Holy Spirit is in us. We too have access to that same life-giving powerful source through Jesus Christ. We won't cower when we know who we are and who are enemies aren't. Think of depression as an enemy, addiction as an enemy. Sickness and disease are enemies. Sin is your enemy. When your enemies come against you, they are coming up against God. When depression or cancer strikes you, it is coming against the child of God. You have to remember who you are and what is yours by right. You are in a covenant relationship with Almighty God. He is your God, and you are his child. We can be like David and remember or like the rest of the nation who cowered and shrank back in fear in the face of the enemy. Cancer is our enemy. Lift up the shield of faith against it.

Listen to how David spoke to Goliath in 1 Samuel 17:45-47. We need to speak the same way in the face of Goliath. We have a choice to believe like David or believe like the rest of the Israelite army. Do we believe God cares about us in this life or not? Do we believe God has left us alone or that he is our ever present help in time of need (Psalm 46:2)? Declare like David did. SPEAK LIKE DAVID DID to the Goliath coming against you.

David Says:

"Today the Lord shall deliver you into my hand; I will strike you down and cut off your head. This very day I will feed your dead body and the dead bodies of the Philistine army to the birds of the air and the beasts of the field; thus the whole land shall learn that Israel has a God (1Sam 17:46)."

We Say:

My Lord and savior Jesus Christ has delivered me from _____. I will strike you down _____ and cut off your head. This very day I will give the dead body of _____ to the birds of the air and the beasts of the field and all of my family and friends will know that my God cares.

"You come against me with sword and spear and scimitar, but I come against you in the name of the Lord of hosts, the God of the armies of Israel whom you have insulted (1 Sam 17:45)."

SPEAK to whatever is coming against you. SAY.... You _____ come against me with fear, symptoms and sickness but I come against you in the name of the Lord of Hosts, my father and my Lord Jesus Christ. You have insulted me and I am his child and that means you have insulted him.

"All this multitude, too, shall learn that it is not by sword or spear that the Lord saves. For the battle belongs to the Lord, who shall deliver you into our hands (1Sam 17:47)."

The battle belongs to the Lord and he is our defender, our deliverer and our ever present help in time of need.

VICTORY IS IN THE BATTLE - David Part 3

1 Samuel 17:47 *All those gathered here will know that it is not by sword or spear that the Lord saves; for the battle is the Lord's, and he will give all of you into our hands."*

David said, " The battle is the Lord's, and He will give all of you into our hands." The name of the Lord is mighty to save. Don't lose hope. Be like David and declare it ahead of time. David didn't just show up unprepared. The Bible says David spoke to his soul. *"Why are you downcast, my soul; why do you groan within me? Wait for God, for I shall again praise him, my Savior and my God"* **(Psalm 42:6).**

Your turn, speak like this....
"I am well because I trust that my Lord Jesus has heard my prayer and is going before me." "I am trusting in my Savior Jesus who saved me from sin and has also rescued me from this present danger or circumstance as well. My hope is in Him so that I can expect victory every time."

Get your mind off of you and your failures and sinfulness and get your mind on Jesus and his goodness and his forgiveness. When you praise and start speaking to God, your mind will follow. Faith will rise up in you. Keep your mind and thoughts and heart on him by praising him. This is how we fight evil. PRAYER, WORD, PRAISE, DECLARATIONS, EUCHARIST.

We battle not in the flesh but in the spirit. This is a spiritual battle, and the power is in our confession of faith. Our words are powerful. They can kill, destroy or heal and save. What are your words declaring? What are your thoughts saying? Sometimes it is only when we get aggressive spiritually that we can rest. It increases our faith as we go to his word daily, and remain in the word with prayer, confession, and praise.

THE ARMOR OF GOD - David Part 4

Ephesians 6:10-20 *Finally, draw your strength from the Lord and from his mighty power. [11] Put on the armor of God so that you may be able to stand firm against the tactics of the devil. [12] For our struggle is not with flesh and blood but with the principalities, with the powers, with the world rulers of this present darkness, with the evil spirits in the heavens. [13] Therefore, put on the armor of God, that you may be able to resist on the evil day and, having done everything, to hold your ground. [14] So stand fast with your loins girded in truth, clothed with righteousness as a breastplate, [15] and your feet shod in readiness for the gospel of peace. [16] In all circumstances, hold faith as a shield, to quench all [the] flaming arrows of the evil one. [17] And take the helmet of salvation and the sword of the Spirit, which is the word of God.*

Put on your armor. Our armor is mighty to save because it comes from God. Imagine if we armed ourselves every morning. We have the armor of God available to us, armor that protects us against spiritual forces of evil. Evil forces that want us to fail, hate, remain depressed, lonely, and sick. Put on the armor of God and take your stand, Know what weapons you have like David did and use them. Wield the sword of the Spirit. David didn't have to fight the battle, but he showed up, spoke and the Holy Spirit fought.

2 Corinthians 10: 3-6 [3] For, although we are in the flesh, we do not battle according to the flesh,[4] for the weapons of our battle are not of flesh but are enormously powerful, capable of destroying fortresses. We destroy arguments [5] and every pretension raising itself against the knowledge of God, and take every thought captive in obedience to Christ, [6] and we are ready to punish every disobedience, once your obedience is complete.

The Bible says that David ran quickly to the battle line to meet Goliath. He didn't stop and think about it. He didn't wait till he or someone else talked him out of it. Someone once told me the first thought is from God. The second, third and fourth are from the devil. When you hear from the Lord, go for it. God will direct your paths. He is our guide, and like a rudder, cannot steer a boat that is not moving. Get moving and don't over think it. Just do it, or someone is going to talk you out of it. Know that you are armed. Stay armed and ready every day.

David went against Goliath with five smooth stones, not a huge boulder, not a sword, not a canon, or large artillery, but stones he found in the Wadi (I'm guessing that's the river). He chose river stones, small and smooth; small enough to put in the pocket of his shepherd's bag. That's what killed Goliath. God was the power behind those stones. It doesn't matter how little we know or have, what matters is who we are trusting and believing in. When God's working with us, and through us, even something small will be powerful. Never, underestimate His power or what he can do with you.

WAIT A MINUTE - I AM HEALED

Psalm 118:17 *I shall not die but live and declare the deeds of the Lord*

When I was pregnant with David. I had such bad allergies I was afraid of how I was going to manage. I knew the fall season was coming and I was in trouble because I could not and would not take medicine. I was leading prayer back then in Katy Texas and we would always end each meeting with the squeeze prayer. We would stand in a circle holding hands, taking turns praying out loud. When you were finished praying you would squeeze your neighbor's hand letting them know it was their turn to pray. If you didn't have a prayer request you just passed on the squeeze to the next person. When it came to my turn I prayed for no allergies that fall. We lived in Houston at the time and everyone laughed. I did not get one sneeze that year, not one. It was truly a miracle. I asked in faith in front of everyone and God answered me.

But the following year.....

The following year I did. When I started sneezing I said "wait a minute. I prayed and God healed me. I rebuke you allergies." I said "no way! You can't have me" and I began to fight. See, I knew God had healed me. It was easy to fight because my healing was so obvious and dramatic. There was no way I was letting these allergies back into my life.

For about three weeks the allergies tried to come back and would cause me to itch and sneeze, but every day I reminded them I was healed. I said it every day, and I would pray in tongues as the Holy Spirit taught me, and after 10 minutes they would be gone for the rest of the day, and I would be okay. One day I just got tired of praying, and I began to complain, and God said to me "REALLY, this is too much for you - prayer for 10 minutes is too much?" That very moment my daughter Faith sneezed and I said

"No Lord, forgive me, I am not too tired" and I thanked God. Today all of us are allergy free. The devil will try to rob you of your healing if he can, so at times, it may be a battle but a great battle and one worth fighting because He truly does all the fighting.

Are you in need today? Are you waiting on the Lord? Are you hoping in his goodness? Are you ready for the walls of Jericho to come down? Are you ready for the job to come through for you or yours? If you are waiting for the elusive victory, time to go to battle and the weapons of our warfare are strong enough to demolish strongholds and to destroy the enemy (2 Corinthians 10:4). The weapons we fight with are not physical but spiritual. These weapons include the word of God and praise and worship, so shout today and watch the walls fall like they did at Jericho when the people began to shout.

Don't wait for the victory to begin praising God. Praise Him now for the answer, thank Him now. Declare it done and show God your faith in Him. Praise precedes the victory just like it did for Jehoshaphat in 2 Chronicles 20 or Joshua at Jericho in Joshua 6. Read these stories of how God ambushed the enemies while the Israelites praised God.

So get up and lift up your arms wherever you are and praise God. SING, SHOUT, SPEAK. Let the devil know who you believe in and who is fighting your battles. THIS IS HOW WE WIN. Declare or proclaim your victory like David did. Don't wait until you feel well or see the victory, declare it ahead of time like David did when Goliath came against him with a sword and spear and a javelin. David told him he was going to beat him and kill him. He went on to tell Goliath that he was going to feed his flesh to the birds.

Tell the accuser you are forgiven; tell the nightmares Jesus is Lord; tell depression it's under your feet; tell dementia you have the mind of Christ. Start now.

I am forgiven, My past has been washed away, and I am completely new because I am yours and you make me brand new. I surrender myself to you Lord. I believe you love me and care about me. I trust you; I trust you with my health, my life, my children, my future. I am your child. I am accepted and adopted into the family of God. I am a daughter of the most High God. I am strong in the Lord and in His mighty power because He makes me strong. You Lord are my strength. The Holy Spirit lives in me. Greater is He that is in me than he that is in the world. I am free from blemish, cleansed, holy and blameless in your sight because I am in Christ. I have been saved from God's wrath because I am in Christ, hidden in Him. I have been redeemed. I am His chosen possession. I trust you, Lord. You say you will never leave me and I believe you. I am convinced you love me and are protecting me and keeping me safe. I am victorious. I am an overcomer; I am His child, His heir. I can do all things through you Jesus who strengthens me. I can bend a bow of bronze; I can scale a wall. You are my shield, my hiding place, my strong tower.

Therefore, I declare.... Say out loud..... I shall speak to myself and say....

I am healed. By Jesus' stripes, I am healed. Jesus took my burdens, my sins, and my sickness with him to the cross. I am free. I believe in you Jesus. I choose to believe even though every part of me wants to doubt. My mind, my will, and my emotions want to doubt. But today I am choosing to believe for your sake Lord and for my sake and my family's sake. Father, thank you for sending Jesus to die for me and to take all my sins and sickness from me. Thank you for healing me. It doesn't feel like it, but I believe you are healing me right now, and I will feel better. I believe my ears will hear; my legs will carry me, my back will become strong again, and I will find relief from pain in the name of Jesus. I am saying these things because you say God to believe not in the seen but in the unseen.

"Cancer you are a defeated foe by the blood of Jesus." Acts 10:38 says "God anointed Jesus of Nazareth with the Holy Spirit and with power, who went about doing good and healing all who were oppressed by the devil, for God was with Him."

Deut 28:7 *You, Lord, scatter the enemy and cause our enemies to be defeated.*

Hebrews 2:14 *In as much then as the children have partaken of flesh and blood, He Himself likewise shared in the same, that through death He might destroy him who had the power of death, that is, the devil.*

WHAT ARE YOU THINKING ABOUT

Philippians 4:8-9 *⁸ Finally, brothers, whatever is true, whatever is honorable, whatever is just, whatever is pure, whatever is lovely, whatever is gracious, if there is any excellence and if there is anything worthy of praise, think about these things. ⁹ Keep on doing what you have learned and received and heard and seen in me. Then the God of peace will be with you.*

What are you spending your thoughts on? Where do your thoughts go? If you are thinking or worrying, your mind is on your worries, fears or circumstances. Maybe you are playing something you did wrong over and over again in your head. Maybe you can't get the fear of dying or getting sick out of your mind. Maybe you doubt you were ever saved or healed. God wants us to change our thoughts and keep our thoughts on him. He promises to keep us in perfect peace when we do. How do we keep our thoughts on him? It takes training. The bible calls it renewing your mind in Christ Jesus. I like to call it REHAB. We need new habitual thought patterns. Since this is God's will and desire for us, he provides the way.

1. Read the Bible daily. This is how we keep our mind on Him. This is how we give our mind new things to think about. The word of God is our offensive weapon against the enemy. It is sharper than any double-edged sword. It is meant to be wielded. Speak the word of God. Learn it and speak it. When we speak the word of God we give it power. It has no power remaining in a book. The word of God needs access to your mind and thoughts.

2. Change your Thoughts. Our minds can only think of one thing at a time. The devil will want to keep you thinking his thoughts; you have to change them. God will help you as you come to him and enter into his presence.

3. Speak and Praise God - Your mind is redirected when you start speaking. Tell your thoughts something new. Do it out loud as

often as you can. Tell yourself the truth. You have been living in this world for so long all you know are lies. The Truth has been hidden from you. You were kept in the dark. It's time to shed some light on the subject. God will help you as you come to him and enter into his presence. Spend time praising and singing to him.

AUTHOR MARK WUENSCHEL

I COME BOLDLY AND CONFIDENTLY

2 Chronicles 32:7-8 *"Be strong and steadfast; do not be afraid or dismayed because of the king of Assyria and all the horde coming with him, for there is more with us than with him. ⁸ He has only an arm of flesh, but we have the Lord, our God, to help us and to fight our battles." And the people took confidence from the words of Hezekiah, king of Judah.*

Just like the people of Israel took confidence in Hezekiah's words, we take confidence in God's word. His word builds us up and gives us hope and peace.

But something always robs us of that confidence. Jesus said, "The devil, comes to kill, steal and destroy." He is always accusing us and reminding us of what we have done wrong. He will keep us feeling undeserving and believing we are unworthy. He wants us to beg for mercy, even though mercy was given to us already. God declared us not guilty when Jesus took our sins. The devil though will rob us of that knowledge if he can and keep us in the dark. As long as he can keep our eyes on ourselves, our unworthiness, our sinfulness, our inability to get it right, on our past, we will never know the truth and be set free. Jesus says "and you will know the truth, and the truth will set you free." (John 8:32)

We have an enemy who is jealous of us and our freedom so therefore he wants us to remain bound and trapped and believing him. Nothing has changed. His tactics are the same as they were with Adam and Eve. He can't harm us, but he will distract us, lie to us and scare us if we let him.

Another one of his tactics is to accuse us. There is always something the devil can use against us. If not, he will think of something we should be doing or show us how little we do. Because what we do is never enough. If you prayed 12 times that day, he will convince you it should have been more. So it is not in our works that we gain access to God and his mercy and grace and intervention, but through the blood of Christ.

Jesus is the one who gives us the confidence we need to approach God because he takes away what separates us from God, our sin, guilt, and shame. We have no confidence approaching God without Jesus that is why we always go to the Father through Jesus. Jesus is the way to the Father. The devil doesn't want us to know this, so he will keep us away from God's word and keep us distracted with many things.

Hebrews 4:16 so let us approach God's throne of grace with confidence, so that we may receive mercy and find grace to help us in our time of need.

Jesus became sin for us that we can become the righteousness of God. This is for all who are "In Christ." Jesus made us sinless so that we could go to God with confidence. That is what we are lacking. We lack the confidence to ask in faith, because our sins are always before us instead of where they should be, on the cross. Our confidence is still in ourselves as if one day we will make it; we will become the man or woman God has called us to be. We believe we will make it if we just keep trying; if we just keep striving. We believe that one day we will be good enough to deserve his goodness, his mercy, and his forgiveness. Fortunately for us, we can never become that person on our own and through the flesh. The only way is through the Spirit which we received when we were born anew in Christ. We became new creations in Christ Jesus.

2 Corinthians 5:17 "So whoever is in Christ is a new creation: the old things have passed away, behold, new things have come".

Philippians 4:13 says that we can do all things through Christ who strengthens us.

John 15:5 I am the vine, you are the branches. Whoever remains in me and I in him will bear much fruit, because without me you can do nothing.

Does our sinful nature keep us from receiving God's blessings? Yes! But we are no longer bound by that sinful nature because we have been reborn. As we remain in him and he is us, we cannot keep sinning because we have a new nature. We have His nature. He will convict us and draw us ever more up and out of the flesh and into the spirit.

We have an identity crisis. We don't know who we are and what we have become so we remain without confidence and do not approach God. We need to put on CHRIST, the robe of righteousness and remember who we are. *For he has rescued us from the dominion of darkness and brought us into the kingdom of the Son he loves* (Colossians 1:13).

When we realize that all the promises of God are for us because we belong to Jesus, we have the confidence we need to trust that God is really helping us and fighting our battles for us. Let us approach than the throne of Grace and Mercy and receive our help in our time of need, knowing who we are in Christ. We are sons and daughters of the Most High God.

PRAY THESE SCRIPTURES and gain confidence.

"I am a new creation in Christ, the old 'me' is gone, and I am brand new in him. I am not a slave to the things of this world, God has rescued me from darkness and brought me into his kingdom, and I am a child of God. I can do all things through Christ because he in my strength. Therefore, I come boldly before the throne of grace and mercy knowing this is the desire of my God who sent his son to die for me so that I could do just that. I am strong and steadfast and not afraid or dismayed by what is coming against me. I know that my God is stronger and on my side and fighting this battle for me."

COURAGE DAUGHTER

Matthew 9:22 *Jesus turned around and saw her, and said, "Courage, daughter! Your faith has saved you." And from that hour the woman was cured.*

Many were touching Jesus that day, He was surrounded, yet he felt her touch. Why was her touch different? What saved the woman with the issue of Blood? Jesus said it was her faith. What faith did she have and where did it come from?

She heard about Jesus and believed He would heal her. She didn't hope He would, or wonder if He would, she knew. She said if I just touch His cloak I shall be cured. She didn't say I might be cured. She said, "I will be cured." I want that kind of faith.

It took courage to have that kind of faith and step out into the road, and Jesus knew it. Any woman with a flow of blood was considered unclean whether it was part of her menstrual period or beyond, and anyone she touched was also unclean (Leviticus 15:19, 25). In the Old Testament if a person was unclean they were separated from the rest of the community. If you touched anything or anyone who was declared "unclean" by the priest, you became unclean. You became unclean through contact. No one could become clean by touching someone clean. It didn't work that way. The clean person became unclean not the other way around.

Until Jesus came

Jesus came to bring life. He is the author of life and in Him is life and health. When Jesus touched the leper, the leper was made clean. This was unheard of. Jesus broke the rules. I think the woman with the issue of blood heard these stories; the Bible says she heard about Jesus. News of Jesus touching lepers must have caught her attention. "Maybe the same thing would happen to her," she must have thought. What did she have to loose? Her, "maybe," became the certainty. The more she heard about Jesus, the more she believed. I bet she listened for reports about Him all the time. Then one day she gathered her courage and sought Him out.

Jesus changed everything. The dead were raised to life, the prisoners were set free, the lame were walking, mute talking, the blind seeing, the lepers were made whole, the sinners were forgiven, and the unclean made clean again.

OUR FINAL RESTING PLACE

Matthew 11:28-30 *"Come to me, all you who labor and are burdened, and I will give you rest. Take my yoke upon you and learn from me, for I am meek and humble of heart; and you will find rest for yourselves* [30] *For my yoke is easy, and my burden light".*

I want to share something with you today. Jesus wants to be your final resting place. You have been carrying your burdens long enough. You have been trying to do it on your own for too long. He doesn't want you going it alone. You can't. You don't have the power. You don't have the willpower or any other power to overcome your troubles, addictions or conquer any shortcomings. You don't have the power but Jesus does.

God is not going to let you down, just don't give up on Him. Don't start trusting in something or someone else. Don't panic, rest in Him. Jesus says "Come to me, all you who labor and are burdened, and I will give you rest." Come to Jesus. He is inviting you to come to Him right now just the way you are. He wants you with all the burdens, sins, sickness, and dirt. He wants to unload those burdens and take them away. He does not want to add to them.

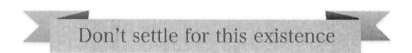
Don't settle for this existence

It is all about Jesus. Jesus loves you today just the way you are. He loves you with all your sins and insecurities, and failings. He loves the mess that you are because He knows it is not the way you really are. He is, if you give Him a chance, going to recreate you in HIS image. People will not recognize you. You will become brand new in His presence, no matter how old you are. Jesus is taking you to new heights, new places in Him. Don't give up; don't settle for this existence, whatever it is. He has a life for you, a TRUE LIFE, a life worth living, a life free from all hang-ups and past hurts and failings.

Stay with Him, don't turn away, your victory is right around the corner, and it is sure. Get yoked to Him; choose His way and not yours. He is the Way, knows the way, and always guides us along the path to freedom and victory. Yoked to Him you will always go the right way, and it always leads to victory in this life and for all eternity.

What is it like to be yoked to Jesus? He tells us His burden is easy, His burden is light. Don't let the devil lie to you and tell you what life with Jesus will be like. Life with Jesus is restful, invigorating and perfect and His instruction is gentle for He is humble.

The verse right before this says, "My Father has entrusted everything to me. No one truly knows the Son except the Father, and no one truly knows the Father except the Son and those to whom the Son chooses to reveal Him." He is the answer! There is no other answer, God said so. When Moses took his time coming down from the mountain where he was meeting with God, the Israelites did a terrible thing. They made a calf of gold and worshiped it. They offered burnt offerings to it. It was such a horrible sight that when Moses saw it, took the tablets of stone, on which God, with His very own hand had carved the Ten Commandments, and threw them on the ground, breaking them. Three thousand people died that day. It doesn't take much for people to hope in other things, believe in other remedies, or turn to other gods. Don't stray and don't grow weary, remain steadfast in your hope in God alone.

Be confident that God is doing a work in you and in all your circumstances. It will get better, just hold on. He never goes back on His Word, and He promises in His Word to protect you and take care of you. You are His child. This will pass. Psalm 34 says *"he delivers from ALL fear, saves from ALL trouble, and those who seek Him lack nothing."* God honors His Word to those who believe it to be true and trust Him.

LIFE IS IN THE BLOOD

Leviticus 17:11 *for the life of the body is in its blood. I have given you the blood on the altar to purify you, making you right with the Lord. It is the blood, given in exchange for a life, that makes purification possible.*

God made us to be one with him from the beginning but Adam and Eve chose to live on their own and away from God, outside of the Garden of Eden. They were placed in a spectacular garden of paradise. Even with everything, they would ever need or ever want they still broke God's covenant with them which was to keep away from the Tree of Knowledge of good and evil. Sin has separated us from God, but God made plans for a way back to fellowship with him through his son and the cross on which he shed his blood.

God told Adam and Eve that if they ate from the tree of the Knowledge of Good and Evil, they would surely die. They chose death instead of life in the Garden of Eden. They chose to obey the serpent instead of God. Death was their inheritance and original sin entered the world through Adam and Eve. We inherited the sin nature but God chose to restore us and all of Adam and Eve's descendants to life through Jesus, and it began with animal sacrifices. The blood from the animal sacrifices was payment for the sins of the people, a life for a life. This was all a foreshadowing of the true blood sacrifice that would be payment for our sins. God exchanged the life of Jesus with ours through the shedding of his blood.

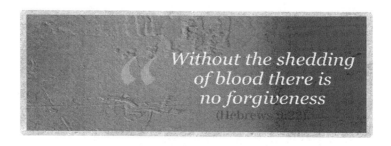

Without the shedding of blood there is no forgiveness
(Hebrews 9:22)

God made Abraham into a mighty nation, and they became God's chosen people through bloody circumcision which is a sign of the covenant God made with Abraham and His people. When God freed the Israelites from Egypt, He did it with the blood of the lamb. God sent the Angel of Death to destroy the firstborn of everyone one in the land. The angel of death spared every family who had the blood of the lamb on their doorpost. The Angel of Death passed over that home, and "Passover" was celebrated annually from that night on as a remembrance of how God saved His people, Abraham's descendants, from slavery (Exodus 12). Moses set up through God's instruction a priestly system of burnt offerings to the Lord where the animals were slaughtered and burnt upon the altar at the tabernacle morning and evening every day. This went on for thousands of years.

The blood sacrifice was a way for the sinner to go free while an innocent animal was offered as a sacrificial substitute. The animal became sin. All the sin of the guilty party was transferred to the animal and was called a sin offering (Leviticus 4).

2 Corinthians 5:21 He made Him who knew no sin to be sin on our behalf, so that we might become the righteousness of God in Him.

Jesus is the Lamb of God, the true Lamb of God who came to earth for us, to be our sacrificial lamb and to take our sins from us so we could be guilt free and live. Just like the Israelites had the blood of the lamb on their door posts we too have the blood of Jesus covering us and cleansing us from all our sins because we have entered into a new covenant with God through the blood of His Son Jesus. Jesus saved us eternally forever once and for all. The prior sacrifices were only a foreshadowing of the one true sacrifice to come. The Bible says that the sacrifice of bulls and goats could never make us perfect, but only Jesus makes us perfect and frees our consciences of sin. Hebrews 10:4 says *"for it is impossible that the blood of bulls and goats take away sins."*

We are totally free, permanently free, and forever free. There will never be the need for another sacrifice.

The Old Testament offerings were simply a constant reminder of their sins. It was a reminder of their condition and need for a savior. God called for the blood sacrifice of animals because He was teaching His people about the cost of sin. When the Israelites sinned under the Old Covenant, God required the blood of goats, lambs, and bulls so we would know just how horrid sin was. Sin required death.

Romans 6:23 the wages of sin is death but the gift of God is eternal life in Christ Jesus. Since we were all sinners we all deserved death.

1 John 1:8 If we say that we have no sin, we are deceiving ourselves and the truth is not in us.

There is no more sacrificing. Jesus is the final sacrifice. The old covenant ended at the cross. The Passover celebration became the Supper of the Lamb, our celebration of the Eucharist. The Bible says that Jesus is the fulfillment of the law. Jesus was the end all. He came on a mission of salvation and on the cross He said "It is finished," eternal life was won for us that day. He did it all for us. Just for us.

God chose to save us from death. Sin required death, Adam and Eve chose death. We get the opportunity to choose once again for ourselves - LIFE. Life comes through Jesus Christ. Jesus restores us to full fellowship with God as our Father, and that fellowship begins now, right now.

We can come to the Father right now and always "IN CHRIST." In Christ Jesus, we are fully alive and have eternal life because His blood cleanses us form all sin that we might live life to the fullest. We can't stand on our own in front of the King of Kings. We were never meant to. We were always meant to be one with God, and He made us one with Him through His Son Jesus who is the way to the Father.

Ephesians 1:7 In Him we have redemption through His blood, the forgiveness of our trespasses, according to the riches of His grace

Matthew 26:27-28 And when He had taken a cup and given thanks, He gave it to them, saying, "Drink from it, all of you; for this is My blood of the covenant,
which is poured out for many for forgiveness of sins.

Ephesians 2:13 But now in Christ Jesus you who formerly were far off have been brought near by the blood of Christ.

GOD DOESN'T SHOW OFF

Psalm 18:1-3 *I love you, Lord; you are my strength.² The Lord is my rock, my fortress, and my savior; my God is my rock, in whom I find protection. He is my shield, the power that saves me, and my place of safety. ³ I called on the Lord, who is worthy of praise, and he saved me from my enemies.*

God's word describes God as our rock, our fortress, our deliverer from all our enemies, and savior. God is not a man that he should lie, nor is he trying to trick us or confuse us. God doesn't tell us how great and powerful he is just to show off. God tells us this because he wants us to know it and rest in him, trust him and dwell in him, free from all worry, striving, depression and fear.

Deuteronomy 33:26 *There is none like the God of Jeshurun, who rides the heavens in his power, who rides the clouds in his majesty;*

Revelations 1:8 "I am the Alpha and the Omega, *the* Beginning and *the* End," says the Lord, "who is and who was and who is to come, the Almighty."

He doesn't tell us how great and powerful he is just to Lord it over us. He tells us of his greatness, so we will know of his protection and run to him. God calls himself our strong tower, and he goes on to say the just run to it and you are safe. (Proverbs 18:10).

This isn't for a select few but for all who call on his name.

Romans 10:13 *For "Everyone who calls on the name of the Lord will be saved."*

God wants us well. God tells us he is "our healer" because he wants to heal us. He doesn't play games. Why is that so hard for us to believe God wants us well. I think because we believe if we are suffering it is somehow holy, and beneficial for someone else. Holy Suffering is this, love the husband God gave you, love your parents, your neighbors, boss, or those you meet every day. Give to those in need. Holy suffering is loving those you find hardest to love. Forgiving the unforgivable is the suffering God calls us to; suffering for his name's sake.

Suffer by telling someone about Jesus no matter how they may treat you or reject you. God may call you to visit the sick and suffering, lay hands on the sick, or suffer persecution for Jesus's sake. Even then he promises to be with us and bring us through. He does not want us to suffer just for the sake of suffering. There is no redeeming value in that. But be like Epaphroditus, Paul's brother, and co-worker, who for the sake of the work of Christ came close to death, risking his life (Phil 2:30).

God says " CAST ALL YOUR CARES ON ME BECAUSE I CARE FOR YOU" 1 Peter 5:7. God didn't say I own the cattle on a thousand hills so he could show off how great he was and watch us do without. He didn't tell us to ask him for anything over and over again so he could play mind games with us. He really does care for you and me.

KEEP YOUR EYES ON JESUS

Psalm 18: 16-19 *He reached down from heaven and rescued me; he drew me out of deep waters. [17] He rescued me from my powerful enemies, from those who hated me and were too strong for me. [18] They attacked me at a moment when I was in distress, but the Lord supported me. [19] He led me to a place of safety; he rescued me because he delights in me.*

You may be going through hell but you are not the first, and if you keep hanging on to Jesus you will get through this. This too will pass. It will not last just don't give up believing. Jesus is still the answer. There is a Rodney Atkins song that used to play on the radio and part of it went like this "If you're goin' through hell keep on going. Don't slow down and if you're scared don't show it. You might get out before the devil even knows you're there." Don't worry you are moving and you are coming out even though it seem slow. This battle is worth the fight because you are coming out of it higher, stronger and better. You are just learning some battle strategies along the way.

Do not worry. There is nothing this devil can do to harm you. He can only scare you. That is his weapon of choice, and that is his tactic. He wants you dependent on him not on God. He wants to separate you from your source and your protection. He likes to get us alone, away from Christian friends and the church. Don't let the devil keep you from church, Bible study or prayer group. He wants your guard down.

The devil always tries the hardest and screams the loudest right before your victory and his defeat. Don't give up when it's almost yours. Be immovable and unshakable, and the devil won't even bother you. When you are standing on solid ground, he cannot shake you.

His tactics are to get you to look at him, look and be overwhelmed by your situation or problem. He will keep you focused on the problem. This is the time though to put your eyes on Jesus. Once you start recognizing the enemy, it's so much easier to stand firm. "Oh it's just you again," you will say, "I have heard that before. Oh, you think you can plant those memories and thoughts and get me to doubt my husband's love for me or thoughts of hatred and annoyance?" When you recognize the enemy start rejoicing, the victory is yours. It gets easier and easier. You become wiser and wiser in God's presence.

GET YOUR MIND OFF OF YOU AND YOUR failures and sinfulness and get your mind on Jesus and his goodness and his forgiveness. When you praise and start speaking to God, your mind will follow. Faith will rise up in you. Keep your mind and thoughts and heart on him by praising him throughout the day. Praise him daily before you get sick, before trouble comes, before you run into situations that cause you to sin. Be purposeful and prepared.

GOD HEALS EVERYTHING

ISAIAH 53:4-5 *Yet it was our pain that he bore, our sufferings he endured. We thought of him as stricken, struck down by God and afflicted, ⁵ But he was pierced for our sins, crushed for our iniquity. He bore the punishment that makes us whole, by his wounds we were healed.*

This Old Testament prophet Isaiah is prophesying about Jesus. This is the scripture that Matthew quotes regarding Jesus. Matthew is talking about how Jesus is healing everyone, and then he tells us that this is to fulfill what Isaiah the prophet said, "He took away our infirmities and bore our diseases." Matthew uses infirmities and diseases because that is what the Hebrew words mean in Isaiah 53. If you were to translate the Hebrew word "choliy," 80% of the time in the bible it meant physical healing and Matthew confirms this. In verse five, Isaiah says he was pierced for our sins, crushed for our iniquity and he bore the punishment that makes us whole and ends with "by his wounds, we were healed."

"By his stripes, we were healed." This is a powerful verse, and the devil hates that we know this verse. The word of God, coupled with faith is victorious over the enemy every time. By his wounds, we are healed physically, mentally, emotionally, and spiritually. Our whole being, body, and soul are healed by Jesus. He cares about all of us. Our soul is our mind, will, and emotions.

Just what does God heal through the wounds of Jesus?

cancer	alzheimer's	ALS
dementia	alergies	ADD
scoliosis	blind/deaf/dumb	you name it

144

Everything imaginable, what do you want him to heal? What have you asked him to heal? What are you believing and trusting him to heal?

If you lived with Jesus you would have seen the mute speaking, the deformed made whole, the lame walking, and the blind able to see, the lepers cleansed; the deformed made whole, and the crowds glorified the God of Israel. Jesus healed the sick, cast out demons and raised the dead and he tells us in John 14:12 that we too if we believe in him, "will do what he does and will do even greater ones than these because he is going to the Father." Verse 13 continues with "And whatever you ask in my name, I will do, so that the Father may be glorified in the Son. If you ask anything of me in my name, I will do it."

We can quote these scriptures from Isaiah and Matthew and make it our prayer.

"I am well because Jesus heard my prayer and has healed me. He took my infirmities and carried my disease. By his Stripes I am healed. Thank you Lord for healing me; for taking this burden from me."

IT IS IMPORTANT TO WANT TO BE HEALED

Believe it or not Some people do not want God to heal them or at least not enough to ask for it.

I met someone a while back with a terminal illness, and when I asked them if they wanted God to heal them, they said: "Hmmmm, I am at peace with whatever God wants." A woman I knew in Houston said "I am on disability. If God heals me, I may lose my disability and have to go to work." Not everyone wants to be healed.

Some people do not want to ask God to heal them fearing it won't happen and then what. We don't want others to think we don't have enough faith. What if it doesn't happen? Then what? What will others think of me then?

Usually, when I ask someone who is ill if they want me to pray for them to be healed they will say "I prayed and whatever the Lord wills, that is what I want. I am just trusting God. He will do whatever he wants, and I am at peace and fine with that." It sounds so holy, so right, so humble. We elevate these people to sainthood. We too want to be like them. We salute them. The problem is they are missing it. God's will IS to heal. I find this hard to write this because I fear you can't comprehend God's love and desire you personally. It's so easy to doubt healing is coming. It's just too hard with the evidence stacked against it. That is what robs our faith. The evidence against the healing.

It takes faith to believe it's God's will to heal you. It doesn't take faith to believe he might not. Most of us believe that God may not. We have seen too many people get sick and die. We see a lot in this physical natural world and it's east to believe what we see and hear and read about in the news whether it is directly opposed to God's word or not.

You have to know who you are and what God has promised you. You have to know what the covenant provides for you and the word of God says. The covenant that God made with you through Christ includes not only forgiveness but healing as well. These are gifts and not earned. God doesn't distribute them based on your good works but to all who trust him as God and Father. Healing comes to us through God's mercy and grace. When you realize it's all based on what Christ did and not what you did or do or have done, it makes it easy to receive the gift and believe God wants to heal you. When you look at you and what you have done or do or are capable of doing, it's impossible to believe God would ever do anything for you or me.

But God doesn't do it for us. He does it for Jesus. Jesus is the one who earned the right for us to be healed and forgiven. He paid the way. He is the reason we are forgiven not us. We are forgiven and healed because Jesus took all the punishment meant for our sins. Jesus wants you healed because he loves you. Everything God and Jesus have done is out of love, pure love for you and me.

We don't deserve it and never will. Nothing we ever do can make us worthy. Jesus makes us worthy. He gets all the glory. And he did it for us because he loves us. He doesn't have favorites. If Jesus heals Sam, he will heal Mary. If he heals Mary, he will heal Sam.

It's just pride or vanity that keeps us from admitting we need faith. We just plain do. Why is it so hard to admit you may need faith to believe. We would rather blame God or interpret scripture our own way than admit we just don't have enough faith or we let doubt sneak in and steal our faith. We can't do it alone; we may not have faith alone, but together we believe. We need each other. When one of us is down another is up. When our faith is weak another's faith is strong. Our lack of faith is good news. When we recognize our lack of faith, then we will know that there is faith to be had and we will run to the Word of God and fill up on faith. If you are sick read scriptures over and over again about healing and you will see your faith in God grow. (SEE APPENDIX for the List of Healing Scriptures).

When Jesus said in Mark 11 "when you pray, believe that you have received it and it will be yours," he meant it. When Jesus said "whoever says to this mountain 'go throw yourself into the sea' and believes that what he says will happen, it will happen for him/her exactly as he/she said it would," he meant it. You just have to be willing to believe God will do it for you. It's hard, impossible in fact because everything in the natural world is fighting against your faith.

The Canaanite woman did not say whatever you wish Lord. If she did, she would have missed what God had for her. Blind Bartimaeus, when asked by Jesus what he wanted, said: "Rabbi, I want to see." He didn't say I want the strength to get through this or money or a place to live and people to care for me. He said I want to see you and Jesus said: "Your faith has healed you." Immediately he received his sight. We are so afraid God won't, we don't dare ask.

Healing is a choice, your choice. God already made a decision to heal you. Healing is his will for you. This is the good news. You may have to walk through this for now, but God has you and is bringing you through if you want it and are willing to persevere in faith.

RIVERS OF LIVING WATER

John 7:37-39 *On the last day, that great day of the feast, Jesus stood and cried out, saying, "If anyone thirsts, let him come to Me and drink. 38He who believes in Me, as the Scripture has said, out of his heart will flow rivers of living water." 39But this He spoke concerning the Spirit, whom those believing in Him would receive; for the Holy Spirit was not yet given, because Jesus was not yet glorified.*

Have you ever wanted something say to eat or drink, but you just couldn't put your finger on what that it was? You go to the fridge standing there with the door open looking in to see if anything grabs you. You are hungry for something, but you just don't know what?

Our souls can get like that too. We get restless and crave something but don't know what it is. We are thirsty for something, but for what? Thirsty, we desire refreshment.

Our bodies are made up of about 80% water. If you are running low on fluids, your body sends you a signal, hey I'm thirsty! Could be dry mouth, thick tongue, headache, in some cases fatigue. It lets you know you are lacking something. Our souls do the same thing. A dehydrated heart, inner man, sends you signals too. Spats of anger, anxiety, fear, irritability, bad attitude, frustration, stress, and sickness. You know you need something you want something but what?

You may be thinking well that is just a part of life, a part of who I am. Some people have high blood pressure, some people have marital problems, struggling through life is just normal, me I fret. I'm a fretter that's what I do. And moodiness? Everybody has THOSE days. Sometimes you are just down, these feelings are inevitable right? Well yes, they will come. But are these thirsts unquenchable? Are the challenges of life unconquerable? NO WAY.

Take a big gulp. Of what you may say? Jesus answered this question one October day in Jerusalem. It was the annual reenactment of the water from the rock miracle that Moses performed while in the dessert. People packed the city. They honored their ancestors by staying in tents; they were nomads out in the desert. And they paid tribute to the desert stream by pouring water out on the altar.

Picture Jesus watching this re-enactment where water is being poured out onto the altar. He is watching them pour water in remembrance of when God quenched their thirst in the dessert. John 7:37-38 says "On the last day that great day of the feast Jesus stood and cried out saying If anyone thirsts let him come to ME and drink. He who believes in Me as the Scripture has said out of his heart will flow rivers of living water." One translation(NLT) said, "he stood and shouted." He was commanding their attention. He was saying why are you doing this ritual when the living water is standing right here. DRINK OF ME! He is saying to you why are you sitting there thirsty I AM RIGHT HERE DRINK OF ME. What are you hungry for, what are you thirsting for? He is your answer; he is your living water. Drink of Him. He has all that you need.

Prayer starter: Lord help me to drink of you. You alone can satisfy my thirst, my hunger, my need. You and you alone are the answer. You have given your all to me. And I receive your gift now Lord. I believe that you are living waters to every dry place in my life. You are greater than anything that I face. Your grace is sufficient and overflowing, and your love for me is beyond my comprehension and never ending. Your word says rivers of living water, not only are you my supply today but each and every day you have what I need. I drink of you Lord. And I receive the life you freely give me.

Thank you, Father, for being more than enough and for being more than I could ever possibly need. You are an endless river in the dessert and my path in the wilderness. There is no end to you, and nothing is too difficult for you. You are faithful, you are mighty, you are awesome, and there is no end to you. Nothing I face, nothing I do, can ever exhaust your supply of grace, mercy, love, joy, peace, healing, provision, power, and life. You are the great I AM. The Alpha and Omega. Glory, honor, and praise be to your name. In the matchless name of Jesus, I rest in you. Amen.

AUTHOR CRYSTAL HEXAMER

YOU ARE HIS MASTERPIECE

Psalm 139: 13-18 *You formed my inmost being; you knit me in my mother's womb.*[14] *I praise you, because I am wonderfully made; wonderful are your works!*

Gentlemen this one is for your wife or daughter. Read this with her in mind. You are the man in her life for a reason. Let her know how beautiful she is. If we don't hear this from our father or our husband we will seek out someone else.

WOMAN!

God wants you to know that this scripture if referring to you, you are fearfully and wonderfully made. God saved his best for last. He created woman last. She was his final work of creation, his masterpiece. God made us perfect. God made you gorgeous. You are a work of art. Believe it. Believe the truth; God is telling you the truth, everything else you hear that contradicts this word, this message to you from God, is a lie. The problem is we have believed the lie for so long we believe the lie to be right and true and God's word just a fairytale, meaningless words to try to make us feel better about ourselves. In fact, the word of God is the absolute truth. I am praying that as you read this, you believe that you are wonderfully made like Psalm 139 says you are.

In the Garden of Eden, Eve listened to the devil and believed what he said. We listen to all the messages on the television about how we are to look, and we believe them. We listen to what the world says and every time we do we will be disappointed. No matter how rich and famous or beautiful you are, there will always be someone prettier or more talented. No matter how hard we try, we will never measure up. It's impossible to measure up to a woman on television that spends hundreds, maybe thousands of dollars and hours and hours of makeup and hairdressing to look just a certain way for the camera for only one second. Then they doctor up the photo to make it even more "perfect." No one looks this way in real life, and we aren't supposed to. It's not beautiful. It's phony.

When someone tells us we are ugly, we should cut our hair, we can't sing, we are worthless and will never amount to anything, we believe them. Like Eve, we are easily seduced and easily mislead. When there is a void in our life, the devil will find a way to creep in, fill the void. He will tell you there is something better out there, somewhere, maybe on the next tree, when nothing in this world will ever satisfy.

If you don't believe you are gorgeous, it's because you are listening to that crafty devil, that snake in the garden out to rob you of your true glory, your true beauty, your true you. He wants to destroy you and your honor and position. Read this again and again until you believe it!

We believe what the world wants us to believe. This was Eve's problem. She believed the devil more than God. She listened to and hung out with the snake and believed what the snake told her about God and about herself. She believed a snake. We as women have done the same.

Who are you listening to?
Who are you following?
Who are you taking advice from?
Who are you hanging around?
WHO ARE YOU BELIEVING?

When we hear someone tell us by their words or actions that we are ugly, unimportant, or worthless, we feel rejected, neglected, overlooked. We believe what they say about us more than what God says about us. God says we are perfectly and wonderfully made.

The problem is not what we look like but who we are believing. The only reason you believed the people who made fun of you was because the devil wanted you to believe them. He hates you and who you are and what you are to become. He wants you to stay in the muck, stay in the pit. But we are rising up and out. We are brand new in Jesus Christ as of right this minute, right now. We are choosing Christ this very moment. Repeat after me. I choose to believe You Lord Jesus and your word. You are the way, the truth, and the life.

God made heaven and earth and everything in it. Each day he made something and at the end of the day he said: "It is good." When God Made humans He said, "It is very good." He was so pleased with us - but we still care more about what the snake thinks.

REST IN JESUS

Genesis 2:24 *That is why a man leaves his father and mother and clings to his wife, and the two of them become one body.*

God created man and woman to be together, to be fruitful and multiply. Adam and Eve were made for each other, made to need each other and made to be together. God made Eve from a rib he took from Adam so a part of him would always be missing without Eve. Eve also is not whole without Adam's rib. Marriage, the union of husband and wife, is a picture of our relationship with God. In the same way, Adam and Eve are not whole without each other; we too are not whole without God. God made us this way on purpose. We can't live without Him. We were never meant to live without Him.

Not everyone has a husband here on earth, but we all have a husband. God is our husband.

Isaiah 54:5 *"For your husband is your Maker, Whose name is the LORD of hosts; And your Redeemer is the Holy One of Israel, Who is called the God of all the earth.*

This verse is important. If we don't get this, we will live our lives always missing something, never whole, never feeling good enough, pretty enough, complete, or smart enough. We will live life unfulfilled if we are not united with our Creator. We will never be complete if God is not at the center of our lives. Whether man or woman we simply are incomplete and going nowhere without God. You may think you know where you are going, but in the end, you will find that the whole time you were climbing that ladder of success, your ladder was leaning on the wrong building.

God made us to need him. Just like God made Eve to need Adam and vice versa we too are always missing something if we don't have Jesus. We try to fill the hole, the emptiness, with anything and everything but the problem is we are looking in all the wrong places. God made us to need him because he doesn't want us to be apart from him. We were made to walk together through life, step by step united.

We are never satisfied till we rest in Jesus. Jesus is our home, our resting place. Without him we are restless. There is always something more to do, to become, we keep thinking ourselves as incomplete, unproductive, unfinished till we find rest in him. He makes us whole, fills us and completes us. He is our resting place.

Without Jesus at the center of our lives, we can do nothing. We become nothing. My friend once told me that without Jesus, I can do nothing. I thought, that's not true you can do something. Everyone can do something.

But listen to what God says in John 15:5 *"I am the vine, you are the branches. Whoever remains in me and I in him will bear much fruit because without me you can do nothing."*

Without Jesus we are nothing, we can do nothing, we are good for nothing. Verse 6 of John 15 goes on to say *"Anyone who does not remain in me will be thrown out like a branch and wither; people will gather them and throw them into a fire and they will be burned."*

Without Jesus, we become what we make of ourselves. We become formed by who and what we listen to and follow. If we aren't following Jesus, we are formed into the image of what we are believing and whoever we are listening to or following.

HE MAKES US

Hebrews 12:2 *fixing our eyes on Jesus, the author and perfecter of faith*

God can handle our sins and wicked behaviors. God can overturn every curse or plan formed against us and can rebuild what the devil has destroyed and what we have destroyed. All he needs is us to be on his team; in his kingdom. All he wants is you, and he wants you just the way you are, sins and all. He can deal with you and all your insecurities, your past, your anger, your hatred, your rage, and your addictions. He has a way of washing us clean and bringing a sweet smelling aroma out of decay and garbage. God can restore us and make us brand new if we are willing and if we persevere.

The ride may be bumpy, and it may feel like you aren't making any progress at all but hang in there, and you will see everything turn around in your favor as you remain in Him. He will do the work in you as you remain in the Potter's hands.

I remember when I was raising my children I would fly off the handle and slam the door, scream and yell and slap a child. I would feel miserable afterward and come crawling to God for forgiveness wondering when would I get better. Why was I not growing in this area? Why did I keep failing? The Holy Spirit wasn't finished with me. Some things about us he changes immediately and other things over time. Even though I was baptized in the Holy Spirit, I needed to learn how to walk in the Spirit daily and to practice walking in the Spirit. I needed to be praying in tongues when the going got rough and counting on him. Years later I would look back and be amazed at how far I had come.

Don't quit, don't worry, it's coming. When you are in the thick of it keep trusting, keep doing good, keep hanging on.

The devil is out to kill you, steal from you and utterly destroy you. You can let him or take what he has meant for harm and put it in the Holy Spirit's hands. He will form out of it a masterpiece. He promises. He is constantly guiding us, directing us.

Who are you? Are you one of God's beloved? Yes, you are! Do you love God and are you called according to his purpose? You wouldn't be reading this if you were not. Don't let your thoughts tell you otherwise. Those thoughts are from the evil one who wants you to think you are unloved and on your own. Remind yourself who you are. Speak it out loud. This is very powerful, and over time, you will believe it to be the truth. It is the truth because it's God's word regarding you.

Speak to yourself and say...

> "I am called by God. I have a purpose and God has a special plan for me. He knows me and has prepared me for work in his kingdom. I am a child of God. I am made in the image of Jesus and God is continuing to mold me into his image. I am born again into new life in Christ. The spirit of God dwells in me, and the light of the world shines through me."

If you said that and continue to say it, you will begin to believe the truth about who you are.

GOD EQUIPS THOSE HE CALLS

2 Timothy 3:16-17 *All scripture is inspired by God and is useful for teaching, for refutation, for correction, and for training in righteousness, so that one who belongs to God may be competent, equipped for every good work.*

One day I called my friend Pam and asked her to pray for me. I was speaking to a group of women and felt overwhelmed. I was afraid this wasn't my calling and began to have doubts about teaching. I began to have those thoughts, "did I prepare enough, was I really called to do this, what are people going to think of me? Am I going to fail and fall flat on my face and make a fool out of myself, are people going to take me seriously, is God going to show up? Am I doing this for him or for me?" Pam said to me, "Marybeth you are such a good speaker." When she said that to me, I heard God telling me to start declaring the same thing about myself. I knew at that moment I was supposed to start speaking to myself. I told myself immediately

"I am called to teach God's word.
I am anointed to do it.
I am a good speaker."

I began to speak to myself, and I felt stronger and actually forgot my fears altogether.

God does not call those who are equipped, but he does equip those he calls. Moses stuttered but lead the Israelite nation into the desert and through the wilderness for over 40 years. Peter was a fisherman and unfaithful yet through the power of the Holy Spirit, 3000 people joined the church the very first time he spoke. With God all things are possible. The Bible says in Mark 9:23 that *"everything is possible to one who has faith."*

GOD TURNS EVERYTHING TO GOOD

Romans 8:28 *We know that all things work for good for those who love God, who are called according to his purpose.*

Some of us have had horrible things happen to us in the past. We wonder why God would look the other way? Why did God leave us or allow such a thing to happen to us? Today is the day you hang on to God's promise that he turns all things to good for those who love him. It's not over! You are still living. Expect God to work miracles for you. Hold him to his word. He loves when we hold him to his word. It means we have faith in his word. You are not the same person you were back then. Today you have faith. Today you are walking out from under the curse. Satan may have had his way in the past but today is a new day.

Just because he had you trapped in the past doesn't mean it has to be that way in the future. Let go of those bitter thoughts and feelings. Don't let him have any more ground than he has already taken.

You are God's beloved. Do not doubt it. Today is a new day. Everything the enemy did to you, everything that was meant to harm you, every word spoken against you, God turns and uses for your good. There will come a day when all that has happened to you will be but a memory.

BE "OTHERS" MINDED

2 Corinthians 1:3–7
3 Blessed be the God and Father of our Lord Jesus Christ, the Father of mercies and God of all comfort, 4 who comforts us in all our affliction, so that we may be able to comfort those who are in any affliction, with the comfort with which we ourselves are comforted by God.

Our thoughts are continually on ourselves. We can become consumed with our own needs and desires, and Jesus wants our focus off of ourselves. He wants our thoughts to be his thoughts and our focus toward others.

Today remember others especially those who are sick and fighting disease, pain, and trauma. Remember those who are lost, enslaved and want to kill themselves. Remember those who are battling fear, worry and depression and your fears and worries will pale in comparison. When the Holy Spirit brings someone to mind lift them up to the Lord right there and then. No matter what you are doing, there is always room for a prayer. If it is just a prayer of remembrance.

When your back starts hurting, remember everyone with back pain and lift them up to the Lord. When you are overwhelmed with depression, spend time in prayer for others and watch it lift. When you pass by someone's neighborhood and you know they are sick or battling something pray for them as you drive by. Be as bold as you have faith for. Prophesy to dead bones and say "dead bones live." As we get older we just simply feel that it's time for us to shrivel up and waste away and get sick. But God promises us long life and abundant life. So pray for your back and your bones and then command them to hear the word of the Lord and rise up and be nourished and live and thrive in the name of Jesus. God told Ezekiel to prophesy to the dead bones. Prophesy to the dead bones in your body or your family, church, etc. Say" Rise up and hear the word of the Lord.

Let your everyday events remind you to pray. Pray for those you visit on Facebook or the one you are texting

When we are healed, let's spread the word and pray for and minister to others. God wants us blessed and for us to be a blessing.

GOD IS BEYOND GENEROUS HE IS EXTRAVAGANT

Romans 8:32 *He who did not spare his own Son but handed him over for us all, how will he not also give us everything else along with him?*

God is beyond generous; he is extravagant. This is God speaking to us, and he wants us to know that he will do anything for us. If God gave us Jesus why would he withhold anything else from us? Nothing compares to Jesus. If he gives us Jesus, he will give us anything. God gave us a gift that is priceless, beyond measure, the life of his son Jesus. His blood was shed for us to purchase for us freedom from hell, damnation, and all condemnation. There is no way we could ever pay for it or earn this freedom if we lived a million lives. God knew that all along and did it for us because he loves us unconditionally, just the way we are.

Let's think about this verse and what it says. God sent his One and only Son to earth to die for us. He handed Jesus over to evil for our sake, and if he would do this, then there is nothing he won't do for us. He especially wants to give you healing. Jesus died on the cross to give it to you and me. We have such a hard time believing God wants to heal us yet that is the one thing he already gave us when he went to the cross and he tells us this explicitly in Matthew chapter 8:16-17. *When it was evening, they brought him many who were possessed by demons, and he drove out the spirits by a word and cured all the sick, to fulfill what had been said by Isaiah the prophet: "He took away our infirmities and bore our diseases."*

Because of this promise we can and should go to the Father, and ask Him for our needs.

You may say, "I ask God for things all the time. I ask and ask and ask." May I suggest that maybe you are begging, not asking? Asking the Father is something we do expecting to receive. Begging is what we do expecting not to receive. Begging is asking from a place of undeserving or uncertainty. Begging is for those who are loved conditionally or believe they are loved only when certain conditions are met. We ask because we are loved unconditionally. Jesus made us worthy to receive what we ask for by cleansing us from all our sins, past sins, present sins and future sins. It's hard to believe God is so good, isn't it?

God is not holding anything against you. He can't. How, can he hold this sin of yours, which you can't forget, against you if he already made Jesus pay for it? Quit hanging out with your sin. It's time to release the sin and the guilt and shame that goes with it and hang out with Jesus. When you release it, you too will go to the throne of grace and mercy with expectation, because you go knowing Jesus paid the price that gave you the right to go. You will go boldly and confidently because you know that you go to the Father through Jesus Christ and he remembers your sins no more. There is no record of all your wrongs because they are on Jesus now, not you.

Jesus made us brothers and sisters. Jesus made us his very own. God loves it when we believe that and he actually expects us to believe we are privileged, precious and important to God.

GOD DECIDED TO HEAL LONG AGO

Romans 11:29 *for the gifts and the call of God are irrevocable.*

God is the giver of all good gifts, and He never takes them back.
Rest assured today that God who healed you will sustain you and
protect you from cancer both now and forever. Once God gives he
doesn't take back. God doesn't change his mind. Do you know that
God gave Jesus to you and by this, He proves his love for you
forever? He made a decision to save you from your enemies a
long time ago, over 2000 years ago, when he sent Jesus to earth to
die on the cross. God rescued you from all evil and all darkness
and all sin and all the consequences of sin through his Son Jesus.
God sent Jesus to save you from everything including cancer and
especially from its return.

If you were healed from cancer, then don't let the devil rob you of
your testimony. Hold on to it. Remind yourself daily that you
were healed. Remind the principalities of darkness by declaring
who you are and what is yours.

Declare today:

"The blessings of God are mine.
I am his precious child, his favored possession.
Healing is mine because God healed me and I will not give it up.
I am healed.
It is mine forever.
God's gift to me is irrevocable.
No devil or sickness is going to steal it from me.
I am holding on to what is mine, to what God has given me.
I know my Savior lives.
My savior took the cross for me, he was whipped and bled, and by
his stripes, I am healed, and I stand to testify.
I choose to believe more in Him and his word and his promise
then what it looks like or sounds like."

We don't have to wait until we are sick to declare the healing blessings of God. Begin declaring them right now. What are you afraid of getting? Declare God's healing. What have your family members told you, you would probably get? What have you heard and believed all these years? What is in your past or your ancestry? What disease did your parents or grandparents suffer or die with and now you are afraid of getting? Cancer? Alzheimer's? Dementia?

Our declarations do not move God, but our faith sure does. Our trust in him moves God to act on our behalf. God cannot resist our faith.

Hebrews 11:6 *But without faith it is impossible to please him, for anyone who approaches God must believe that he exists and that he rewards those who seek him*

So speak like you believe it declare:

"I am born again, and no weapon formed against me can prosper. I have the mind of Christ. Jesus is commanding his angels to protect me, so I have nothing to worry about. My bones are strong and healthy; my eyes are bright, and my mind is alert".

Our words build us up. Our words cause faith to rise up in us. Words are powerful. With a word the heavens and earth were created. Jesus sent forth his word and healed them. Jesus is the Word of God made flesh. You and I have the same authority. Jesus says we get what we say.

"Truly I tell you, if anyone says to this mountain, 'Go throw yourself into the sea', and does not doubt in their heart but believes that what they say will happen, it will be done for them" **(Mark 11:23).**

Our words can also tear us down and bring death and destruction. The Israelites when they were in the desert said "Why is the Lord bringing us into this land only to have us fall by the sword? Our wives and little ones will be taken as spoil. Would it not be better for us to return to

Egypt" (Numbers 14:3)? And God gave them just what they declared. *"So tell them, 'As surely as I live, declares the Lord, I will do to you the very thing I heard you say"* (**Numbers 14:28**). God allowed their bodies to fall and die in the desert. When you want to complain and speak negatively be careful, you just may get what you are complaining about. Don't complain about your house. Never say "I hate my house, I hate me....." Be thankful and see the good things about your home, children, husband and expect only better things to come.

Choose to believe God is working for you and not against you. Believe that God's word is true and powerful and speak his word over your life. God's word says this in Jeremiah 29:11 "For I know well the plans I have in mind for you—(says the Lord) - plans for your welfare and not for woe, so as to give you a future of hope. Say that. God is saying that to you right now. Repeat it with your name in it as if he is saying that directly to you.

SAY THIS:

"GOD has a plan for my life. I am on his mind. He is thinking of me. His plan for me is good because he wants the best for me. He has a good healthy future in store for me, one full of hope."

We hear the opposite all day, and we listen to the thoughts the enemy sends our way. It's time for us to introduce new thoughts and penetrate the old habitual thoughts and negative thinking with good thoughts by changing the way we speak to ourselves. Our minds and thoughts will follow our words.

Declare every day that you are cancer free and healed, and the blood of Jesus covers you and protects you. Don't let cancer sneak up on you and threaten and scare you. Be ready for those lies with the word of God on your lips. Stay in God's word and declare his goodness and thank God ahead of time and all the time.

ITS ALWAYS YES!!

2 Corinthians 1:20 *For no matter how many promises God has made, they are "Yes" in Christ. And so through him the "Amen" is spoken by us to the glory of God.*

The Bible says that the promises of God are yes and amen in Christ. Because Jesus took all our sins and became a curse for us, we get all the blessings. We get them not because we are perfect but because they were won for us through Christ.

God's promises are "Yes and Amen." The promises of God are not "yes" then "no." They're not "I don't know" or "Maybe so." The promises of God are "Yes!"

Will He save you? "Yes!"
Will He heal you? "Yes!"
Will He deliver you from every evil? "Yes!"
Will He set you free? "Yes!"
Will He supply all your needs? "Yes!"
Will He take care of you in your old age? Yes!"
Will He provide for you so you lack nothing? Yes!"

The promises of God are "Yes," and the promises of God are "Amen." Who do these promises belong to? They belong to all who are willing to believe and accept them as a gift to us from God the Father through Christ our Lord. They belong to you who belong to Christ.

In the Old Testament, the promises were many times tied to an impossible condition of perfection which we could never attain. But, Christ came and became the perfect one who could, in fact, keep every condition the promise was attached to.

Some promises are conditional

Deuteronomy 30:8-9 You will again obey the Lord and follow **all** his commands I am giving you today. [9] **Then** the Lord your God will make you most prosperous in all the work of your hands and in the fruit of your womb, the young of your livestock and the crops of your land. The Lord will again delight in you and make you prosperous, just as he delighted in your ancestors,

Deuteronomy 30:10 **If** you obey the Lord your God and keep his commands and decrees that are written in this Book of the Law and turn to the Lord your God with **all** your heart and with all your soul.

Deuteronomy 28:1 "Now, **if** you diligently obey the voice of the Lord, your God, carefully observing **all** his commandments which I give you today, ..."

Jesus fulfilled the impossible condition of obedience for us. It is impossible for any of us to observe all his commandments. We fail, but He never failed to obey. He came to the earth to obey for us. In him and through our faith in him and the work he did for us on the cross, we are made perfect, righteous, and holy. It is because of Jesus that we are made worthy of all God's promises

Colossians 1:12-13 *giving thanks to the Father, who has made you fit to share in the inheritance of the holy ones in light. [13] He delivered us from the power of darkness and transferred us to the kingdom of his beloved Son.*

Jesus did it for us. He came to become sin so we could become righteous (holy and clean) and receive the reward of the righteousness. We aren't righteous in our own self. We are wretched, every one of us, but in Christ, we are made perfect and whole. Jesus not only makes us that way but keeps us that way as we remain in him, attached to him like a branch on a vine. We have to find him, live in him, follow him and remain in him. Jesus cleanses us and makes us white as snow but for some reason, we can only see our sins. We see ourselves as soiled and unworthy even though He went through a lot of pain and suffering to make us clean. He makes us worthy to receive all good gifts from God.

God's promise to us who seek him....

Food, shelter and clothing - **Matthew 6:25-34**
Everything - **Romans 8:32**
Deliverance from all trouble - **Psalm 34:20**
Peace - **Philippians 4:6-7**
Future - **Jeremiah 29:11**
Joy - **Nehemiah 8:10, Galatians 5:22**
Rest - **Matthew 11:28**
To Care for us - **I Peter 5:7**
Our children will not beg for bread - **Psalm 37:25**
He will never forsake us - **Psalm 34:10-11**
He will sustain us on our sick bed - **Psalm 41:4**
Healing – **Exodus: 15:26**
Prosperity - **Deuteronomy 28:3-6, 8-12**
Help in time of need - **Phil 4:19**
To rescue us - **Psalm 34:11**
Protection from evil - **Psalm 91, Deuteronomy 28:7**
Defend us - **Psalm 34:5**
Save us - **Acts 16:31**
Forgive us - **Psalm 103:3-4, 12**
The Holy Spirit - **Isaiah 44:3**

All of these promises are for us now, not in the world to come. We don't need healing, provision, safety in heaven. The streets are made of gold; there is no crying or suffering in heaven. God promises to care for us now on earth. We will not walk this earth alone. He is with us, and he promises to be with us, not just when we are good, but always.

Believe he is the God who sent His Son to die for you just the way you are. Believe he is the God who sent His Son Jesus to take away your sins and sickness.

HE BECAME SIN

2 Corinthians 5:19 *For God was in Christ, restoring the world to himself, no longer counting men's sins against them but blotting them out. This is the wonderful message he has given us to tell others.*

Do we have to suffer from the consequences of sin? Are we stuck with what we have made for ourselves? Do we have to sleep in the bed we made for the rest of our lives? If we smoked cigarettes, do we have the right to expect healing from lung cancer or are we doomed? A consequence is something we deserve attached to something we did. Dictionary.com says "the effect, result, or outcome of something occurring earlier."

In Him (JESUS) we can rise above anything. In Him we are free from all the burdens, curses, and consequences of sin because he, Jesus, became a curse for us according to Galatians 3:13. The Bible says that *He became sin that we might become the righteousness of God in Christ Jesus.*

For He made Him who knew no sin to be sin for us, that we might become the righteousness of God in Him. ***2 Corinthians 5:21:***

We are the righteousness of God because we are in Christ Jesus. There is no other reason. We can't earn it. We can't make ourselves right with God. It is a free gift. This is so hard for us to believe and receive and accept. It takes faith.

There is no salvation through anyone else, nor is there any other name under heaven given to the human race by which we are to be saved." ***Acts 4:12***

...giving thanks to the Father, who has qualified you to share in the inheritance of the saints in light. ***Colossians 1:12***

There is therefore now no condemnation to those who are in Christ Jesus, who do not walk according to the flesh, but according to the Spirit.

Romans 8:1

We can walk in the flesh and reap the benefits of the flesh or walk in the spirit and reap the benefits of a spirit filled life. It's up to us. His way leads to all that is good and healthy and rewarding. Walking in the flesh leads to anger, bitterness, jealousy, competition, fear, worry, etc. When we sin we open ourselves up to whatever the devil has for us. I remember once having no compassion for my husband when he was sick. I said to him something like "really, you are going to lie around all day." The next day I was sick.

The Bible says we reap what we sow. I opened myself up for sickness to come right in. It was as if I was saying "come and get me." I have since come to my senses. I reached out to God and asked for mercy immediately. He doesn't hold anything against us, and he didn't hold that against me. God is not out to punish us but to grow us up and discipline us because he has only our best interest at heart all the time. God is good – all the time. The consequences of sin are something we had to bear outside of Christ. The Bible says the wages (consequence) of sin is death, BUT the gift of God is eternal life in Christ Jesus (Romans 6:23).

GOD IS FOR US NOT AGAINST US

1 Corinthians 1:30-31 *It is due to him that you are in Christ Jesus, who became for us wisdom from God, as well as righteousness, sanctification, and redemption, so that, as it is written, "Whoever boasts, should boast in the Lord."*

We are his children, his precious ones. He is not waiting for us to fail so he can pounce on us and punish us. He is committed to us succeeding because in him is only success. In him are victory and blessings, prosperity and favor. In him are grace and mercy. God didn't send his son to this earth so you could live a miserable existence full of doubt, worry, fear, and hopelessness. If our hope is in our very own selves or in our ability to be good, then that would be a miserable, hopeless existence. We will never get it right so we will never know from one day to the next if God is for us or against us. Praise God our hope is not in ourselves but in Him. He wants us to know this, so we will always know that God is for us, on our side.

Are You in Christ? Do you question it all the time? Do you want to know for sure? Many of us go our whole lives wondering if we belong to him or not. We question it every time we sin, and we wonder if God still loves us. Can we still expect his mercy and grace, his healing and all of his blessings? It is hard for us to believe in such a good God. We want to work for it. It's our nature. We can't accept his love because we think it should be earned; we need to feel productive, worthy. We enjoy earning it because it makes us feel good about ourselves. Yet our salvation is not dependent on ourselves or our good deeds.

Let me ask you a few questions. Who saved you? Was it Jesus? Is he your savior or is it you who did the saving? If Jesus saved you, then you are saved because he does a good job. He is the one who rescues us; we can't do it ourselves. All we can do is call on him. The Bible says in **Acts 2:21 "and it shall be that everyone shall be saved who calls on the name of the Lord.'**

The bible even goes on to say that not only does he begin the work in us, he finishes it; he brings it to completion (Hebrews 12:2). He does it all. All we do is pledge our allegiance to him, believe in him and remain in him. We cannot boast of anything. He is the one who does the work in us, chipping away at us and pruning and molding us in his image.

Does this hold true for those outside of Christ? No. They still walk in condemnation because they have not chosen Jesus Christ. Jesus is the way, the truth, and the life and no one can come to the Father without Jesus. Those who do not choose Jesus Christ, choose to remain in darkness tossed to and fro. I did not say this God did. "

John 3:18-20 *Whoever believes in him will not be condemned, but whoever does not believe has already been condemned, because he has not believed in the name of the only Son of God. And this is the verdict, that the light came into the world, but people preferred darkness to light, because their works were evil. For everyone who does wicked things hates the light and does not come toward the light, so that his works might not be exposed."*

Do not remain in this world when you have the opportunity to live and reign in the supernatural. Choose Christ!

STOP DROP and ROLL

2 Corinthians 10:3-5 *For, although we are in the flesh, we do not battle according to the flesh, ⁴ for the weapons of our battle are not of flesh but are enormously powerful, capable of destroying fortresses. We destroy arguments ⁵ and every pretension raising itself against the knowledge of God, and take every thought captive in obedience to Christ,*

Are you overwhelmed today, juggling too many things, and you feel like no one can or will help you? Do you feel oppressed? Oppression is the feeling of being heavily burdened, mentally or physically, by troubles, adverse conditions, anxiety, etc. When we are oppressed we feel out of sorts and we don't know why. The devil would like to keep us this way and make this our way of life. But praise God we have been given the victory, the enemy has been defeated. We just have to recognize him and drive him out.

Think of oppression as a spirit. The Bible says to submit to God, resist the devil, and he will flee. Don't just hang out and let it grip you and keep you. When we know where those feelings and thoughts come from, it's easier to resist. The devil wants to keep us this way forever, so the sooner we start battling, the better. How do we battle?
Try this, **Stop, Drop and Roll.**

STOP - what you are doing and take 10 minutes to read God's word and let God minister to you. He never ever wants you overwhelmed and in a pit of despair.

DROP - to your knees or get on your face before God. Change your position right now. Lift your hands to the Lord, kneel or lay prostrate before him.

ROLL - ROLL - Do something. Don't drag your feet. Don't wait, run, don't walk and get help. What are you waiting for? Call on him, call out to God. Sing, praise God, thank God, start proclaiming the goodness of God. Read the Psalms out loud. Pray scripture, start praying in tongues, call a friend, go to Mass, run into the chapel. Do something. Don't just let yourself go with the flow. Think of yourself on fire or under attack and STOP DROP and ROLL.

If you are at work, start praying in tongues, or find a scripture you have memorized. Start saying it to yourself or out loud if you can over and over again. Say the Our Father or the Glory Be. Sing a praise song. Let the devil know who you are, and who you belong to. Start memorizing Psalms like "The Lord is my shepherd, I shall not want; he makes me lie down in green pastures." "The Lord is my light and my salvation, whom shall I fear." "Even though I walk through the valley of the shadow of death I will fear no evil, your rod, and your staff, they comfort me. I will not fear the terror of the night, nor the arrow that flies by day, nor the pestilence that stalks in the darkness, nor the plague that destroys at midday. No harm will befall me; no disaster will come near my tent for He will command his angels to guard me in all my ways."

There is power in the word of God. The word of God is our offensive weapon against the enemy who wants you off your game and out of his way. He is the one that wants you depressed, scared, worried, oppressed.

The devil is relentless, so you have to be too. You are more than a conqueror through Christ Jesus. But to know this, we have to get our minds off of us and onto him. Take your mind off of you. The devil wants you focused on you. He wants you consumed with you and your thoughts. Remember they are just thoughts, and they aren't your thoughts. Put your hands on your head and command those thoughts into obedience to Jesus and then just keep going. Don't dwell there get busy. Start praying for someone else or go do something for someone. Start a project, just don't be alone with your thoughts. If you are hanging on to Jesus I have good news for you; you are coming out on the other side. It may not seem like it but don't trust what your eyes see or what your thoughts and feelings are telling you. You are a conqueror through Jesus Christ.

Pray God's Word.

God's word is a weapon against our enemies.

God's word says....

- I will remove sickness from your midst; - **Exodus 23:25**

- I am the Lord who heals you. - **Exodus 15:26**

- And the Lord will protect you from all sickness. He will not let you suffer from the terrible diseases you knew in Egypt, but he will inflict them on all your enemies! - **Deuteronomy 7:15**

- He forgives all my sins and heals all my diseases. - **Psalm 103:3**

- When it was evening, they brought him many who were possessed by demons, and he drove out the spirits by a word and cured all the sick, to fulfill what had been said by Isaiah the prophet: "He took away our -infirmities and bore our diseases." **Matthew 8:16-17**

- He bore the punishment that makes us whole; by his wounds, we were healed. **Isaiah 53:5**

- For we walk by faith, not by sight. **2 Cor 5:7**

You and I PRAY ....

God has removed sickness from my midst. God is my Lord who heals me and he will protect me from all sickness. He will not let me suffer from terrible diseases because he forgives all my sins and heals all my diseases. Jesus took away my infirmities and bore my diseases including _____ (Place your hand on _____ if you can). He bore my punishment and makes me whole and by his wounds I am healed. I walk by faith and not by sight.

GOD'S RIGHTEOUSNESS vs SELF RIGHTEOUSNESS

2 Corinthians 5:21 *For our sake he made him to be sin who did not know sin, so that we might become the righteousness of God in him.* **Romans 5:19** *so through the obedience of one the many will be made righteous.*

You are righteous (free from sin and guilt, morally right with God) because you are in Christ Jesus and he makes you righteous. You are not righteous in and of yourself that is self- righteousness. You are righteous before God through Jesus Christ and through him alone. He took sin and gave us his righteousness. He is our righteousness.

Self-righteousness - makes us feel good about ourselves when we do something right.
God's righteousness - makes us good when things are going right or wrong.

Self-righteousness - makes us feel bad about ourselves when things are not going right.
God's righteousness - is not based on feelings but the truth about ourselves when things are going right or wrong.

Self-righteousness - depends on our own goodness.
God's righteousness - depends on his goodness, not ours.

Self-righteousness - makes us feel puffed up and better than others when we succeed or do a good deed.
God's righteousness - causes us to do good deeds for God's sake, not ours.

Self-righteousness - is shaky ground. We never know where we stand, one-day good, next day bad.
God's righteousness - is solid ground. We always know where we stand. God doesn't change his mind about us based on our failures or successes.

Self-righteousness - depends on the past.
God's righteousness - is directed to the future giving you everything you need to overcome sin, and addiction.

Self-righteousness - says I failed and have to do better.
God's righteousness - says I failed and God's mercy, grace, and power are with me to bring me higher.

Self-righteousness - keeps us focused on ourselves and our actions.
God's righteousness - keeps us focused on him and his power to bring us through.

Self-righteousness - makes other's failures intolerable.
God's righteousness - makes us merciful and forgiving.

Self-righteousness - You get all the glory when things go well.
God's righteousness - God gets all the glory when things go well.

Self-righteousness - You get the blame when things go south.
God's righteousness - God takes the blame and the consequences.

YOU HAVE NEW DNA

Galatians 3:13-14 *Christ has redeemed us from the curse of the law, having become a curse for us, for it is written, "Cursed is everyone who hangs on a tree", ¹⁴ that the blessing of Abraham might come upon the Gentiles in Christ Jesus, that we might receive the promise of the Spirit through faith.*

All generational curses no longer have authority over you. The only reason they exist and flourish is because we don't know the authority we have over them through Christ. They have been allowed to not only remain but flourish and passed on from one generation to the next.

We invite the curse to remain every time we talk about it as if it is ours as if we own it. Don't accept dementia just because it runs in the family. It stops running in the family today. Don't accept Alzheimer's or cancer as if you are doomed just because your mother had it or your grandmother or great grandfather. I don't care if all of them had it, it's assignment against you has been broken. The Bible says that people perish for lack of knowledge (Hosea 4:6). How true. When you take authority over it, the authority given to you by Jesus - it is over, and it is not being passed to your children. Let's be the one to protect the future generations. It takes work. It takes faith. The devil will not give up easily. He is relentless. The devil is not going to roll over and play dead. You have to be more relentless in your faith and your words.

You are not who your ancestors were. You do not share in their diseases, even those diseases that are genetic. We have been graced with a new DNA. I am telling you the truth, and I am going to show you how I know it to be true. *"Jesus came that we might have life"* (John 10:10), not just life in heaven but life now on this earth. He says I came that they might have life and have it abundantly. Jesus obviously cares about our physical lives. His healings while on earth testify to his desire to see us well. The devil, on the other hand, came to destroy, rob and kill us.

In the Old Testament or under The Old Covenant, the curse came to all who disobeyed. The curses were, among other things, sickness and disease. These curses lasted for generations. Have you ever noticed a family where the mom has anger issues, and so does the daughter and the grandmother? Anger and rage seem to run in the family. Or a father who has depression and passes it down to his daughter and grandson.

Exodus 34:7 *I lavish unfailing love to a thousand generations. I forgive iniquity, rebellion, and sin. But I do not excuse the guilty. I lay the sins of the parents upon their children and grandchildren; the entire family is affected—even children in the third and fourth generations."*

Sin is generational. Because of our father Adam we all received the "curse" of original sin. It was handed down from generation to generation.

Today God excuses the guilty through Christ and Christ alone. He is our way out of generational curses. We do not bear the sins of our parents. We have been forgiven of all sins and, therefore, the curses can no longer attach themselves to us. This is good news to all who have been burdened under the yoke of the "inevitable" and "certain" genetic disorders our parents have or had. Did your mother, and her mother and her mother's mother all have Alzheimer's or Dementia? Do you fear you too will get it or are cursed with bad genes? Does Breast Cancer or Rheumatoid Arthritis run in your family? It may, but someone somewhere has to take a stand against its attack. Take a stand against the disease wreaking havoc in your family tree, if not for your sake then for the sake of your children and their children and their children's children. Make for yourself a new legacy, a new heritage. This is your right in Christ, your covenant right.

When Jesus took the cross, he became a curse for us because the bible says everyone who hangs on a tree is cursed referring to Jesus' crucifixion, which set us free from the curse of sin and it's punishment. Merriam-Webster defines a curse as evil or misfortune that comes as if in response to imprecation or as retribution.

In Numbers chapter 21, the Israelites complained to Moses, speaking against God and wishing they had just remained as slaves in Egypt. The Lord, angry and in judgment sent serpents which bit the people, killing many of the Israelites. The people came to Moses begging him to pray to the Lord asking for forgiveness. God told Moses to make a serpent out of brass and put it on a long piece of wood and lift it up in the air. Everyone who is bitten will live when they look at the brass snake. This is a foreshadowing of Jesus. John 3:14 says *"And as Moses lifted up the serpent in the wilderness, so must the Son of Man be lifted up,"* Jesus was lifted up for us, so we could look at him and be healed.

We have received the curse because we have simply accepted it as a reality in our lives. In the same way, we can receive Jesus as the one who broke the curse and simply accept it as a reality in our lives. Which reality do you want? In Luke chapter, 10 Jesus is sending out the 72 disciples and tells them in verses eight and nine *"Whatever town you enter and they welcome you, eat what is set before you, cure the sick in it...."* Later upon their return, Jesus tells them in verse 19 *" Behold I have given you the power to tread upon serpents and scorpions and upon the full force of the enemy and nothing will harm you."*

When you recognize a generational curse or stronghold, renounce it and be set free. Don't accept it as part of who you are; you have been liberated by Jesus. Jesus said in Mark 16:17 *"These signs will accompany those who believe: in my name they will drive out demons, they will speak new languages."* If you have demons bothering you whether they are generational or otherwise, God has given you authority and the power, as a believer, to cast them out of you.

They only remain because they have not been commanded to leave. Take authority over yourself and your loved ones.

2 Corinthians 10:3-4 *"For, although we are in the flesh, we do not battle according to the flesh, ⁴ for the weapons of*

our battle are not of flesh but are enormously powerful,
capable of destroying fortresses.

The weapons we fight with are spiritual, the Holy Spirit, The
Word of God, the Eucharist, faith and love. All of these
weapons are to retrain us to believe and stand firm. USE
YOUR MOUTH. It is a weapon. We are going to change
what we believe and are trusting in by changing what we
speak. The longer you keep telling your family and friends
that you are going to get dementia because your mother had
it the longer you will believe it and fear i, and it will loom
over you. But if you start speaking that Jesus redeemed you
from the curse, from all sickness and disease like he says he
does, (See Matthew 8:17), you will begin to believe it.
Watch what you say. We believe and eventually become
what we say. SAY INSTEAD My mind is alert. My mind is
strong and healthy because Jesus is Lord of my mind. (See
the back of the book for prayers to fight.)

Ernest Hemingway, not a professed Godly man, was quoted as
saying "I'll probably go the same way" referring to his father who
committed suicide in 1928. In 1961 Ernest Hemingway committed
suicide. His brother and sister also committed suicide. His
granddaughter Margaux, a beautiful fashion model, and actress
committed suicide in 1996. Don't ever say such a thing. You
speak something long enough you believe it and receive it.

A friend of mine just had the doctor tell her that her daughter
had an autoimmune disorder and that it runs in the family.
Knowing it wasn't her family she quickly learned it was her
husband's family and she immediately felt anger toward her
husband. After a day or so she realized that we all have
things in our ancestry that are hurtful or cause pain and
illness. But because we are in a covenant relationship with
God through the blood of his son Jesus, we belong to a
different family with a new ancestry. We are heirs of the
Kingdom of God. We don't have to accept this condition as

generational anymore.   Declare it over your life. Let those new words come out of your mouth.

"My daughter is healed and no weapon formed against her will prosper or be carried to the next generation. My daughter is a child of God, with His blood in her veins. She is a co-heir with Christ. I reject this autoimmune disease and praise God for healing her. My daughter is healed and whole and completely well and set free because Jesus is my Lord and has rescued us from all evil and sickness and disease."

Galatians 4:7 *Therefore you are no longer a slave but a son, and if a son, then an heir of God through Christ.* **James 2:5** *Listen, my beloved brothers, has not God chosen those who are poor in the world to be rich in faith and heirs of the kingdom, which he has promised to those who love him?*

As an heir, we get all the blessings of God, and because Jesus died for us and became a curse for us, we get none of the curses. Declare I am a new creation, born anew in Christ and he is my ancestor. Make a decision and choose life, the abundant life. Do it for your family, the generations to come, do it for God's glory. **Psalm 34:11** *The rich grow poor and go hungry, but those who seek the Lord lack no good thing.*

Pope Benedict —

The world promises you comfort, but you were not made for comfort. You were made for greatness.

I don't think Pope Benedict meant we were never to rest or get comfortable and cozy or snuggle up on the couch. I find I need to do this more often just to let my body and mind rest.

But love takes us out of our comfort zones. God's love motivates us to become more and do more and be more. The Greater One lives in us and his love and anointing burns within us. We find love is a driving force that gets us up and out. That love within us causes us to show up even when it's not convenient, go where we might not otherwise go, do what we never thought possible.

It is not our love that brings us to greatness but his love. We have to first receive his love, and that love will flow out of us to a dry and thirsty world. Is it okay to want greatness? With God in us, how can we be anything but great? We want greatness because greatness is pure, lovely, honorable, noble, just, gracious, and true. We want greatness because we are a reflection of the King of kings, the Maker of heaven and earth. We are his masterpiece, his spokesperson, his ambassador. We live to glorify the Almighty God and reflect his kindness and the riches of his grace (Ephesians 2:7). We are part of the body of Christ and together as one body we reflect his majesty, his greatness, his power and his love.

This is who we were made to be in Christ Jesus and he is molding us and fashioning us. He is not finished with us, but the work he has begun in us he will complete. He is the author and the finisher of our faith (Hebrews 12:2, Philippians 1:6). This is the real us made in the image of God, filled with the Holy Spirit.

Philippians 1:6 *being confident of this very thing, that He who has begun a good work in you will complete it until the day of Jesus Christ;*

GOD IS GOOD

James 1:17 *Every good and perfect gift is from above, coming down from the Father of the heavenly lights, who does not change like shifting shadows.*

Believe it is God's will to heal you.

Once you get this, life is so much better. You can then actually rest in the Lord, knowing he will take care of you. Without knowing his will regarding healing, you will always wonder and doubt whether or not God cares for you. God has only one desire regarding you, and it's always good. "God is good all the time, and all the time, God is good." This isn't just a saying it's the truth. He is good to us now, here on earth. His days of punishing you are over because you have chosen to follow Jesus. You have become his disciple.
                    YES?   NO?

Well, it's time to make a decision for Christ. You have to live in one kingdom or the other. You get to choose. The door is open to those who knock. The door is open. If you are still reading this, you are a disciple already, or you wouldn't still be reading.

Just to let you know. Quit doubting you are with Jesus. He has no doubts about you. He wants you for himself. Everything Jesus ever did or is doing is for you. You are his great reward. You are his prize. You are the reason he came to earth and suffered and died. He wants you both now and forever. "NOW" and FOREVER." He wants you living in his kingdom with him now, not just in the hereafter.

In the New Testament Jesus never turns anyone down. He will not turn you down either, oh you and me of little faith. God's will is to heal you. Always. He always wants what's best for you. He is the perfect parent.

We so quickly believe it may NOT be his will, why not believe it may, in fact, be his will. Believe today and forever that it is God's will to heal you and deliver you from this infirmity or affliction no matter how old you are and no matter how long you have been afflicted.

You have to believe it is always God's will to heal, or you will never believe it is his will to heal you. If you don't believe it is his will to heal all the time, then you will always find a reason why he shouldn't or won't. It's all or nothing. God either heals or he doesn't. Dare to believe God is that good. He either heals or he doesn't. God doesn't heal one and not the other. He is not deciding yes to one and no to another. It doesn't depend on your good works or your sinlessness. If it did, we would never have anything. But just like we can't earn forgiveness, the same is true for healing. We can't earn healing.

If we believe that there is a chance that God may not heal then, we will always believe that that is, in fact, the case at any time. Because we never measure up, because we always have need for improvement, we will always "feel" unworthy of healing so... if there is a shred of doubt that God heals we will take it. When we think to ourselves, "It may not be God's will," we are left relying on our own efforts to win his approval for healing or more likely just settling with the fact that we owe God something and need to pay it and this sickness must be it. When you accept the fact that God's will is to heal you, you are accepting in reality, the gift of God, his son for your very self. You are saying to God, I believe and accept the gift of grace and mercy that you gave the world through your son Jesus. It no longer becomes words you repeat at Mass, but true faith in God.

Dare to believe God wants to heal you. The Bible says that Jesus did God's will on earth and only his will. "For I have come down from heaven, not to do My own will, but the will of Him who sent Me (John 6:38). He did nothing except the will of God. He said only what He heard God say. If Jesus healed on earth than don't you think that it is God's will.

Jesus tells us to go and lay hands on the sick, and they will get well (Mark 16:18). He says ⁸ Whatever town you enter, and they welcome you, eat what is set before you, ⁹ cure the sick in it and say to them, 'The kingdom of God is at hand for you.' (Luke 10:8-9). If God said to do it, then it must be his will to do it. Soon, we who are sick will get healed and start spreading the good news and laying hands on the sick.

I once bought a plaque That said this "Faith is believing not that God can but that God will." I had that plaque on my wall for years speaking to me. Faith is not believing God can. We all believe God can. Even the devil knows God can do anything. God can do whatever he wants. It doesn't take faith to believe God can, but it does, however, require faith to believe God will.

If you are fighting or struggling to believe that God's desire is to heal you, keep seeking and knocking and reading. Hang in there. You will never be disappointed for having too much faith in God or for seeking him too much. It will never be charged against you. Dig deep into God's word. Do it though with the Holy Spirit. The Holy Spirit will never lead you anywhere but the truth.

It is his nature to heal. That is what he does and who he is. God can't **not** heal. God can't **not** forgive. There is nothing he won't forgive. He can't **not** love. He is love. He can't lie or go back on his word.

He is always bringing us up and out. Up from the pit, out of darkness, out of sin, out of hell, out of muck and mire, out of depression, out of illness, He is always healing us from sickness, disease, worry and fear and timidity. He is always bringing us up and out. Where you are now is not where you are meant to stay.

God has no desire to leave you where you are no matter how good or bad it is. He has a higher place in mind for you, a better place and he will spare nothing to lead you there as long as you are willing to follow.

GOD DECIDED YOU WERE WORTH IT

1 Peter 1:18-20 *For you know that God paid a ransom to save you from the empty life you inherited from your ancestors. And it was not paid with mere gold or silver, which lose their value. ¹⁹ It was the precious blood of Christ, the sinless, spotless Lamb of God. ²⁰ God chose him as your ransom long before the world began.*

You may be married to a fool or born to abusive parents or maybe your whole life you were treated unfairly or poorly by friends, siblings or classmates. Maybe you were called stupid or ugly.

How do you live with someone cruel, abusive or hateful?

- Don't let them rub off on you.
- Find God, believe and receive his love and hold on.
- Wait for God. God will do one of two things, change the person or take them out of your life.
- God's love never fails.

When you know God loves you, when you are sure of it, you can endure anything. Nothing can harm you. No one can say anything to move you. Don't value yourself according to someone's opinion of you. You are not defined by what others say or believe about you. Receive your value from God.

Know your worth. What are you worth? What is your value?

You may have a home that you believe is worth $500,000.00 but if no one is willing to pay more than $200,000.00 for it than it's real value is $200,000.00. Value is determined by what people are willing to pay or exchange for something. God paid for us, and the price he was willing to pay was a value beyond measure. You have a value, and it's beyond measure.

You and I have been purchased by the blood of the lamb, ransomed "the Son of Man came not to be served but to serve, and to give his life as a ransom for many" (Mark 10:45). We were ransomed from the death penalty that we earned by sinning. Yes, we all deserve death because of our sinfulness, but God chose to die in our place and secured for us a place with him in heaven forever instead. The Bible says "The wages of sin is death but the gift of God is eternal life in Christ Jesus our Lord. (Romans 6:23).

> ## God decided you were worth shedding his own son's blood for.

God decided you were worth shedding his own son's blood for. You do not determine your own value because you do not know your worth. Even more importantly, others do not decide your value. Your value was determined by the one who paid for you, God. What does that mean? You may ask, "How did God pay for me?" We inherited the sinful life and became slaves to sin but God had a different plan for us. He chose to make the payment for freedom from sin for us and deliver us from the coming wrath (1 Thes 1:10). I Corinthians 6:19-20 says.... *"you are not your own?* [20] *For you have been purchased at a price."* You have been purchased, and the price paid to have you transferred out of the kingdom of darkness and into the kingdom of his beloved son was priceless.

Acts 20:28 *Keep watch over yourselves and over the whole flock of which the holy Spirit has appointed you overseers....the church of God that he acquired with his own blood.*

Ephesians 2:13 *But now in Christ Jesus you who once were far off have become near by the blood of Christ.*

I remember praying for someone, and I said to God, "God if I can exchange places with this precious sister of mine, I would." I remember praying I just want to take this from her and do it for her. Let me take this I know I can stand on your word. She is too young".... and I heard Jesus say. "That's what I want to do. I want to take her place. I did it already. I took this from her. I love her so much I told God I would do it for her. I did it for you and for everyone. I took it all. I wanted to do it just like you want to.

That's what I feel for my children. I love them even more than you do. I love them all." This is what Jesus said. I said wow Lord thank you. I will not rob you of the reward, the blessing, and the glory. It's all yours Jesus. Jesus did for us what we could never do.

I never want to rob Jesus of the joy of saving us, rescuing us. Jesus did it already. He did it. It was so huge what he did that his blood sacrifice covers everyone and anyone who calls on his name. He is the answer, not me, not you, not your grandmother in heaven, but Jesus. Jesus is our advocate, our great High Priest, our redeemer, our savior, our ever present help in time of need. He is our mediator, the one that goes before us, covers us and delivers us from every evil. He is our rock, our fortress, our stronghold, our strong tower, and champion. He is our Lord. He earned it and all glory goes to him because

God greatly exalted him and bestowed on him the name that is above every name[10] that at the name of Jesus every knee should bend, of those in heaven and on earth and under the earth,[11] and every tongue confess that Jesus Christ is Lord, to the glory of God the Father. **(Phil 2:9-11)**

You can't determine the value of your house. The one willing to pay determines the value. You can't determine your own worth. God has done that for you. We determine our value based on how well we perform or what we can purchase. Our position determines our worth or maybe our education or good looks. There is nothing in this world that can increase or decrease your value because your value has already been determined and it is not based on your good looks, your good education, or your good deeds. Our value is not determined by our success or failure. A hundred dollar bill is worth a hundred dollars, no matter what we think or believe or declare, it's still a hundred dollars. Whether it's been used and abused, spit upon or stepped on, it's still worth the same, one hundred dollars. The same is true for you and me. No matter what we have done or what we have been through we are still just as valuable to God as we were the day he made us.

Your value has already been decided, and it's priceless, and it is never going to change. God doesn't change his mind. He isn't wishy-washy like we are. One day we feel good about ourselves and value ourselves well and then other days we fail and sin, and we regard ourselves as devalued. God doesn't say yes to you today and no to you tomorrow. God doesn't change his mind based on your actions or attitude. You are his child on good days and bad. He has decided for you.

GOD DOESN'T NEED CONVINCING, YOU DO

Romans 5:8 *But God proves his love for us in that while we were still sinners Christ died for us.*

Jesus loves you! You don't have to convince God to love you, He already does. God doesn't need convincing, you do. You and I need to be convinced beyond a shadow of a doubt that God loves us. He wants more than anything else for you to believe he loves you. Give this to God as a gift, your faith in His Love. God sent Jesus, his only begotten son to die for you and me. He can't prove his love for you any more than that. He will not. He would have to crucify Jesus all over again every time you forgot or doubted his love. God proved his love for us when he sent Jesus once and for all.

If that doesn't prove his love nothing will.

Romans 5:8 *But God proves his love for us in that while we were still sinners Christ died for us.*

So what is our answer to this incredible display of love for us? Believe he loves you and did it for you. God wants that from you more than anything else you have to give Him. Just believe He loves you that much. So much that He was willing to send His one and only Son to die for you. Believe it today. There is nothing keeping you from receiving God's love for you except you. Jesus already took the cross. He risked it all for you. He had died before he had any guarantee that you would accept His punishment for your sins. Did Jesus die in vain? He died for nothing if you don't accept his death for your sins.

Choose to believe you are worth dying for. Choose today to believe you are worth that much to God. It's a choice. Choose Jesus and believe that He loves you more than life itself. Jesus obeyed God and went to the cross because He too, like the Father loves you. He isn't counting any sin against you. He took all your sins on the cross with him when he died. All of your sins. Yesterday's, today's and tomorrow's sins. So there is nothing keeping you from receiving everything God has for you. If not you, who? Who deserves it more than you? NO ONE.

Can I say one more word? Many times people will say to me. Just keep praying, as if God has to be convinced. God doesn't need me to bother him to get him to heal me. He already wants to. That's what we don't understand. I know it's taken me years of reading the Bible and studying his word regarding healing, to realize that God wants to heal me. He doesn't need to be talked into it. He isn't the one that needs convincing you and I are.

HOW TO STAY FREE

Isaiah 8:10 *"Devise a plan, but it will be thwarted; State a proposal, but it will not stand, For God is with us."*

For those who are in a battle and fighting depression, sickness, cancer, dementia, or other serious illness. The Bible says the plan of the enemy is thwarted and will not stand. If you are trusting God to heal you and are believing you are healed and delivered, then I want to remind you not to let the symptoms tell you otherwise. Don't let the symptoms scare you or make you doubt you are healed.

Read this passage from a book called "The Normal Christian Life" by Watchman Nee. I highly recommend it. He was a prisoner in China for being a Christian. He writes:

"Whatever contradicts the truth of God's Word we are to regard as the Devil's lie, not because it may not be in and of itself a very real fact to our senses, but because God has stated a greater fact before which the other must eventually yield. I once had an experience which illustrates this principle. Some years ago I was ill. For six nights I had a high fever and could find no sleep. Then at length, God gave me from Scripture a personal word of healing, and because of this, I expected all symptoms of sickness to vanish at once. Instead of that, not a wink of sleep could I get, and I was not only sleepless but more restless than ever. My temperature rose higher, my pulse beat faster and my head ached more severely than before. The enemy asked, 'where is God's promise? Where is your faith? What about all your prayers? So I was tempted to thrash the whole matter out in prayer again but was rebuked, and this scripture came to mind: 'Thy word is truth' (John 17:17). If God's Word is truth, I thought, then what are these symptoms? They must all be lies! So I declared to the enemy, 'This sleeplessness is a lie, this headache is a lie, this fever is a lie, this high pulse is a lie. In view of what God has said to me, all these symptoms of sickness are just your lies, and God's Word to me is truth.' In five minutes I was asleep, and I awoke the following morning perfectly well.... We must believe no matter how convincing Satan's arguments appear.... "

The devil is a skillful liar. Jesus said of him in John chapter eight, that when the devil lies, he speaks his native language. He does not only speak lies, but his lies come in all forms of deception even symptoms. We must believe one or the other. Satan's lies or God's truth.

Psalm 18:39 For You have girded me with strength for battle;
You have subdued under me those who rose up against me.

Psalm 34:17 The righteous cry, and the Lord hears and
delivers
them out of all their troubles.

The word of God is powerful and even more powerful than the word of God, is the Word of God coming out of your mouth. The devil cannot stand in the presence of God's word. When we submit to God, the Bible says the devil has to flee. When we submit to God in faith, then cancer, depression, anxiety and it's symptoms must flee (James 4:7). Cancer or dementia cannot remain when you come against it in faith with authority. Watch your faith grow as you speak the truth from your mouth. The Bible says that faith comes by hearing the word of God. So start gathering Bible verses and start speaking them so you can hear them.

Today is the day you take authority over your body and rebuke the devourer and his lies. He is nothing but a liar and tries to get us to doubt.

SAY THIS..... "I reject you pain and fatigue, and I command you off of me in the name of Jesus. I don't come against you in my own name but in the name of Jesus, the one who gave me the right to use his name. I am healed, and my body is obeying God and lining up according to the way it was created; healthy and strong."

Jesus commanded the wind and the waves and commands cancer, and it's side effects and gives us the power to do so also. Cancer, depression, dementia and any illness will remain as long as it has free reign and the invitation to stay. We invite it to remain when we complain or cry, but when we remember what is ours and fight, the stronghold is loosened.

Luke 10:19 *I have given you authority over all the power of the Enemy, and to walk among serpents and scorpions and to crush them. Nothing shall injure you!*

GOD WANTS TO HEAL YOU

God not only wants to heal you but it is his will and heart's desire for you to be well, and thriving. God's will is always to heal you. I say this because it is the truth. God's will is his word. If he said it in the bible than he meant it and he means for you to believe that his word is true and for you.

God wants to heal everyone reading this. In fact, there is nobody God doesn't want to heal. he wants to heal you more than you want him to heal you. One night as I was praying, I began to pray for a young friend who was struggling with sickness. I told God, "Lord let me have it because I know how to fight this devil..." before I could finish, I heard God say "me too, I too want to take her place" I about freaked when the enormity of what he said occurred to me. WOW. Jesus loves us so much he died for us. Jesus loves us so much he did it all for us. Jesus loves you and me so much he stood in our place and received all our sins and sicknesses.

Matthew 8:16-17 When it was evening, they brought him many who were possessed by demons, and he drove out the spirits by a word and cured all the sick, 17 to fulfill what had been said by Isaiah the prophet: "He took away our infirmities and bore our diseases."

He received the full punishment for every sin, those past present, and future so you don't have to. If you are forgiven for all your sins then what sin is keeping you from being healed? Remember there is no sin to big for God except the one you keep. But why keep it if Jesus already died to take it. There is no sin Jesus can't handle so give it to him, confess it and be done with it. You may sin again tomorrow, but let's trust God with all our tomorrows too.

If we don't believe God loves us, we will never believe he wants to heal us. Believing he desires to heal us is our way of proving to God that we have received his love, just like believing we are forgiven shows God that we believe he sent his son to die for our sins. When we accept his forgiveness, we accept his son's death and then Jesus didn't die in vain.

Galatians 2:21 *"I do not nullify the grace of God, for if righteousnesscomes through the Law, then Christ died needlessly."*

Little ole us. We have to believe he loves us as much as anyone else.

STONE OF REMEMBRANCE

James 5:13-15 *¹³ Is anyone among you suffering? He should pray. Is anyone in good spirits? He should sing praise. ¹⁴ Is anyone among you sick? He should summon the presbyters of the church, and they should pray over him and anoint [him] with oil in the name of the Lord, ¹⁵ and the prayer of faith will save the sick person, and the Lord will raise him up. If he has committed any sins, he will be forgiven.*

Are you going through it alone? Are you afraid to ask for prayer? Are you afraid to go to church and ask for prayer? The Bible instructs us to ask for prayer from those who are dedicated to the Lord, from those who have faith in God to heal. Go to your pastor, your priest and ask him to anoint you. It is an act of faith to ask, an act of humility. Your priest or pastor has nothing better to do. This is an honor for them. Don't rob them of the privilege, the blessing and the opportunity to see God move.

Do we have to? No. Do we need to? No, but oh the grace associated with it. Not only do you see God move but the whole church is a witness to the power of God in your life. Your healing just became a witness, a testimony of God's goodness. There is power in the sacrament of The Anointing of the Sick. There is grace for you beyond your understanding. God is allowed to move you, grow you, minister to you and take care of you when you invite him to in such a way.

Let your anointing be a "Stone of Remembrance." In the Bible stones of remembrance were used to remind the people of great moves of God. They would remember him and not become fearful or anxious. These stones encouraged faith as the people were reminded of God's love and faithfulness. In 1 Samuel 7:12, Samuel took a stone and placed it on the ground where the battle was won against the Philistines. Joshua, in Joshua 4:6, told the Israelites to *"take up a stone on his shoulder ..... to serve as a sign among you.."* Joshua wanted the people to see the stones and remember the victory God won for them especially during the bad times he knew would be coming. In the same way, our anointing is a stone(sign) of remembrance. When sickness rears its ugly head, or the report looks gloomy you can remember "Father anointed me" or "my group laid hands on me and prayed for me" and this will help you stand strong.

When fear and worry rise up in you, remember you were anointed. God has healed you, and you have no reason to worry or be afraid. Remind yourself who you are believing in; who you are trusting. Tell yourself...

"NO! I went to church and asked." "Jesus said that everyone who asks receives. I am remaining in faith." I am healed, by his stripes, I am healed, Jesus took my sins and my sickness to the cross, so I am well."

Do we have to go to a Priest or Deacon in order to be healed? Absolutely not. God heals, plain and simple. He already made that decision regarding healing long ago. Sometimes, though, we need each other. Sometimes we need a stone of remembrance to hang onto.

Ask someone to pray with you don't be shy. We all need help when we are sick. When we are well, we are there for others, when we are sick we need each other. Reach out and keep reaching out till you are well. Pray together and expect a miracle. The Eucharist is also a stone of remembrance. Jesus said, *"Do this in remembrance of me."* Do you believe in the power of the Eucharist? Do you believe Jesus carried your sickness and sin with him to the cross? The oil used to anoint the sick is blessed at Mass. In the early church, the people were anointed, not once but repeatedly until they were healed. We should be so believing in the Eucharist, that just partaking is enough to be healed. If only we believe.

GIVE IT TO GOD AS A GIFT

1 Corinthians 2:9 *"No eye has seen, no ear has heard, and no mind has imagined what God has prepared for those who love him."*

God doesn't love you more today than yesterday nor will he love you more tomorrow than he does today. God doesn't love you more when you are good and less when you are bad.

We may do that. In fact, we do. When someone is bad, we treat them as if they are bad. But God is not like us. His standards are not our standards. His ways are not our ways (Isaiah 58:8-9). We think God is like us, so we actually expect him to act like we do. He never gets moody. God never gets frustrated with us.

I had a dear friend tell me once "I just can't believe God loves me." It's hard to receive something from someone you don't think loves you. It's hard to receive love and healing and forgiveness from someone when you don't really believe they care about you and love you unconditionally. If you don't believe God loves you, you won't believe he wants to heal you. You won't accept the gift for yourself. If you don't believe he loves you, you won't believe you are forgiven. Don't wait to feel loved and feel forgiven, just believe you are completely forgiven and loved. If you don't, you will never believe you are worthy of any of the promises or gifts of God. Faith is a decision. I am going to believe God loves me. He can't prove it to you any more than he already has. So it's just up to you to receive his love.

I finally told my friend to just receive it for His sake. You owe it to God to believe he loves you. He gave Jesus for you there is nothing more he can do to prove he loves you. How many sons does he have to crucify to get you to believe you are loved by God?

When we are at the end of ourselves, God calls us to rest in Him. Believe in his love today like never before. May this be the day you increase your faith in your God's desire to care for you, protect you and provide for you. He cares for you here on earth. His goal is not to just get you to heaven. His goal is to bring you to life in him right now. He is not our protector in heaven because we need no protection in heaven. He is not our provider in heaven, we have all we need in heaven. Now is the time to trust him.

Right now wherever you are, lift your hands up to the Lord and say "Lord I choose to believe you love me (whether you do or don't) I choose to believe as my gift to you. So whether or not you love me is up to you God. I am going to believe you do and give my faith to you as a gift."

If God gave his son for us because he loves us and for no other reason, then don't you think the greatest gift we can give God is to receive his gift.

TURN EVERY WORRY INTO VICTORY

For some of us, our time of teaching and helping, intervening and lecturing our children is over. They have grown up and moved out. Some of us have been doing it for so long we don't know how to let it go. While our children may still need us and our wisdom, they really don't want to hear it and we, through the Holy Spirit have to determine when to let it go. It's easy to say, and people say it all the time. Let it go.

But what does it mean to "let it go?" Does it mean just to drop it or does it mean you have to deposit your fear, worry or problem into God's hands trusting him to take care of it and bring it to fulfillment? This is a decision you not only have to make but then keep. This is the hard part.

The reason it is so hard is because we don't really trust God to do it. For example, our desire may be for our husband/wife to go to church and we think, if I don't lecture him/her about it, remind them and lay the guilt trip who will? Well deep down do we really trust God to nudge? Do we trust the Holy Spirit to guide, draw and convict or do we know how to do it better? Our spouses should never hear us nag, or complain and certainly never lecture. They are kings/queens, or at least, they should be treated as such. I know, I know, you think, what they are losers or fat, or stupid, careless, inconsiderate, disrespectful, uncaring, lazy or worthless, but not only should those words never come out of our mouths regarding our spouse, we should never even think them. Love conquers all, heals all and saves all. Love is triumphant and so are you when you choose to follow Christ and lay it down. Watch God do the job.

What are your fears, worries, concerns, and problems? Are your adult children addicted and/or away from God, are you afraid of losing your job, do you have an illness, marriage problems or do your children have marriage problems? Are you fearful of getting cancer?

HOW do we get to the place where we can LAY IT DOWN

PROBLEM	PR
PRAYER	PR
PROCLAIM	PR

PROBLEM:

Define your problem and write it out. This helps if you are serious about letting it go. Don't just say "I am sick, or I need help." Be more specific. My daughter is $100,000 in debt. My husband will not go to church. My son is addicted to drugs.

PRAYER:

Be specific. Don't just say I need peace or Healing. Don't be general, stretch your faith and be specific when you ask. General prayers generally do not get answered. Help me prayers are good when you are a baby and desperate and in an emergency, but you will find God growing you up out of that prayer really soon. Ask! God tells us over and over to ask. Ask like you believe God is listening and wants to answer your prayers.

John 14:12-14 *Amen, amen, I say to you, whoever believes in me will do the works that I do, and will do greater ones than these, because I am going to the Father. [13] And whatever you ask in my name, I will do, so that the Father may be glorified in the Son. [14] If you ask anything of me in my name, I will do it.*

Matthew 7:7-8 *ask and it shall be given to you …for EVERYONE WHO ASKS receives*. What do you want? Remember the blind man? Jesus asked him "What do you want?" Duh. Lord I am blind can't you see? No Jesus wants to hear it from you. This is important. God can't give you what you don't ask for. He can! but more often than not it takes you wanting it enough to articulate it. He wants you to know it's him who is giving it to you. When you deliberately ask for something specific he gets all the glory and honor and credit when it happens. Especially when you tell others what you are asking God for. He wants you to recognize him and praise him for it and pass it on so others will get the message!!!!

Prayer example: Father I ask you to heal my son and deliver him from these drugs that control him and have a hold on him.
Prayer example: Father I ask you to speak to my husband and draw him to you. May he join us at church and hunger and thirst for you.

THERE COMES A TIME WHEN YOU HAVE TO TAKE YOUR PRAYER TO THE NEXT LEVEL. Let's call it Believing prayer. Prayer that has no faith is really no prayer at all. Every prayer needs to be believing prayer.

PROCLAIM: OR DECLARE: This is
extremely important and very rarely done but it is so effective. It brings our prayer to a new level of faith. Proclaim is our speaking out loud the answered prayer as if it has already been answered. This is so important because Mark 11 says this *"Have faith in God,"* *Jesus answered. "Truly I tell you, if anyone says to this mountain, 'Go, throw yourself into the sea,' and does not doubt in their heart but believes that what they say will happen, it will be done for them. Therefore I tell you,* **whatever you ask for in prayer, believe that you have received it, and it will be yours.**

This is your way of showing God you believe you have received what you asked for. Faith and trust are important to God. When we speak "I am well" we are saying it not because we feel or look well but because we believe God heard our prayer and is doing something about it. OUR FAITH is now on GOD BECAUSE WE JUST PRAYED. It is in essence faith in our prayer. It shows God you really believe he is healing you.

When I say "I am well in the name of Jesus" I believe that he is working and I am choosing to walk by faith and not by sight. I also believe in the power of his name and I am reminding God and myself that I am coming to him in the Name of Jesus. This is hard at first but so powerful. For instance, when we ask God to heal our son and deliver him from drugs the last thing we want to do is complain to family and friends how bad he is. Didn't you pray? Don't you believe God is doing something? Just because you can't see him, don't you believe he is working, healing, delivering your son? The woman with the issue of blood said if I only just touch his cloak, I will be well. The stretcher bearers said If only we can get him to Jesus and they went through the roof, The centurion said just say the word. Quit talking like God isn't working or he didn't hear you. Have faith. Show you have faith by what comes out of your mouth.

Example: My son is seeking the Lord. I have faith in God. My son is walking in wisdom and grace and is full of the Holy Spirit and free from drugs in the name of Jesus.

EVERY TIME we declare or PROCLAIM

1. It reminds us that we have prayed.
2. It reminds us that we have laid it down.
3. It reminds us that God is working on our behalf and answering the prayer.
4. It's a reminder that we are trusting God.

It's our proclamation that proves to us and to God that we laid it down and let it go. It takes time and effort and a decision to lay it down. OUR DECLARATION keeps us on track. Our declaration or proclamation reminds us we prayed and proves our faith to God that we believe he heard us and is doing something. Our declaration/proclamation is showing God we trust in him and have more faith in him than in what it looks like. Our declaration shows God we have faith in him and we believe God is working on it. Declare it every day, and you will be reminded that you have prayed, and now it's up to God. Every time you declare it you will be reminded you prayed, Oh Yeah I prayed for this, I am confident God is working on it.

SO NOW SPEAK YOUR PRAYER BACK TO GOD as if it's been done.

Mark 11:22-24 *Jesus said to them in reply, "Have faith in God. Amen, I say to you, whoever says to this mountain, 'Be lifted up and thrown into the sea,' and does not doubt in his heart but believes that what he says will happen, it shall be done for him. Therefore, I tell you, all that you ask for in prayer, believe that you will receive it and it shall be yours.*

Speak like you believe it will happen and eventually you will believe it will happen. It may seem like you are faking it or lying but you are not lying. You just believe in something that hasn't manifested in the physical realm yet. The Bible says that Faith comes by hearing. Every time you declare it you hear it.

PR PR PR - Example:

PROBLEM - Son is addicted to drugs or alcohol

PRAYER - Father I am looking to you for deliverance and freedom for my son. Take this addiction away from him.

PROCLAIM - My son _____ is hearing your voice and turning to you. He is free from this bondage and is walking a new life following you Lord Jesus. He has his right mind and is fully engaged in life. My son is healthy and no longer a slave to _____.

PRAYERS -DECLARATIONS

The Bible says to approach the throne of grace and mercy with confidence and boldness. We come boldly to God with our declarations because of Jesus. We can do this because we come with faith in the name of Jesus. Jesus gave us his name because his name gains us access to the Father and we can ask anything and everything when we come to the Father in the name of Jesus. These declarations are made in faith because we walk by faith and not by sight. We don't have to first see it to believe it. We declare it is so because we believe it not because we see it. Our declarations may seem awkward at first, but we declare them knowing our God is working. Our declarations show God our faith in him. Faith is based not on what we see, hear or feel but what God's word says and the promises it holds for us who believe. The Bible says...

Proverbs 4:22 *For they are life to those who find them and health to one's whole body.*

Ephesians 3:12 "in whom we have boldness of speech and confidence of access through faith in him."

PRAYER FOR THE SICK

PRAYER:

Father, I come to you for help. I call to you for healing my body, for complete healing. Only you know what is wrong, Lord and how to fix it and make it better. Thank you for always being there and for always hearing me. You performed so many miracles when you walked on this earth, hear me Lord and answer my cries for help.

DECLARE:

I declare I am well because Jesus said I could ask the Father for anything in his name and He will do it so that He, the Son, may bring glory to his father. He said, "ask me anything in my name, and I will do it" **(John 14:13-14)**. Because of him, I can boldly declare that I am well because I believe Him and know He is true to His word. I am not afraid to ask. I ask in confidence because even though I don't deserve it, Jesus purchased for me with his blood, the right to come boldly to the Father. Through Jesus Christ and because of him, God is my father. I come in Jesus' name asking for more than I deserve because Jesus died so I could ask for anything. He made the way for me. I receive your love and healing dear God and thank you for healing me.

"Sickness and disease, my God, is greater, my God is stronger, my God is higher than anything you can throw at me."

"I declare Lord Jesus; you took my sins, sickness, and disease with you to the cross where it was nailed for evermore. I accept this gift and believe you did it for me. I choose to walk by faith, not by sight. I believe you are healing me and I do not believe the symptoms or what I feel. I believe you and your word more than the symptoms. Your word says You took our infirmities with you to the cross and you bore our diseases." **(Matt 8:17)**.

FEELING CONFUSED OR OUT OF SORTS

PRAYER:

Father, I lift my eyes up to you. You are the source of my well-being.You are the lifter of my soul. You are my ever present help in time of need. I call to you for clarity of mind and for peace. You ordered the earth into being. You created the universe. You hovered over the chaos. I ask you to cleanse my mind and take away all the fog and confusion. Increase my capacity for knowledge, wisdom, discernment and understanding. I am asking Lord for a sharp mind and one that is active and in perfect working order.

DECLARE:

I speak life to my mind. My mind is alive and fully alert. I am connected to my source which is God alone, and the wisdom and knowledge of God are mine through the Holy Spirit. My mind is alert and sharp and in perfect working order. I have the mind of Christ, and all my thoughts are obedient to him. Thank you, Father, for the gift of the Holy Spirit and for a mind that is in perfect peace because it rests in you

PRAYER WHEN IT'S TAKING
A LONG TIME

KEEP YOUR EYES On Jesus. I know it is tempting to pray for help from other sources, but if you want the breakthrough, there is only one source - Jesus. He wants his Father to receive all the glory. Do like Jesus taught us and go to the Father, through Jesus Christ and by the power of the Holy Spirit and experience a breakthrough. It is coming. Jesus is never late and never early, but always right on time. Today, just praise God and believe and trust that this period of waiting is fruitful and effective.

PRAYER:
Thank you for keeping me safe in you Lord Jesus. Fill me with patience and courage and help me trust you are thinking of me and working for my victory. Help me lord to believe and keep on believing

DECLARE:
You are my rock, my God in whom I trust. Some trust in chariots, others in horses; some trust in the work of their hands or their bank accounts; some trust in the health system; others trust in luck, the lottery or in their 401K, but I trust in the name of the Lord my God. I will wait for you, Lord. I will take courage. I am strong in you and in your mighty power. The greater one lives in me, and I will wait for the Lord and not be moved to doubt and fear.

Psalm 27:14 *Wait for the Lord, take courage; be stouthearted, wait for the Lord!*
Psalm 37:9 *Those who do evil will be cut off, but those who wait for the Lord will inherit the earth.*
Psalm 37:34 *Wait eagerly for the Lord, and keep his way; He will raise you up to inherit the earth; you will see when the wicked are cut off.*

WHEN YOU ARE IN PAIN

Speak if you are feeling pain. Don't declare your freedom and healing once and decide to live with it. - It's a battle so fight till it's over. Whether you are battling sin or moodiness or addiction it's the same thing - you declare and fight. The weapon we have is the word in our mouth which increases our faith.

PRAYER:

Lord Jesus, I ask you to take this pain away from me. Your word says in Isaiah that you took our pain and Lord we are holding you to your word. I receive your gift of healing. I trust you are healing me and bringing me relief from pain.

DECLARE:

I choose to believe you are healing me and taking this pain away. Thank you that my whole body is obeying you and lining up to work properly. This pain is leaving me, and I am free. The pain must obey because I come in the name of Jesus who said I could. He gave me his name and the authority to use it.

Isaiah 53:4 Surely he took up our pain and bore our suffering, yet we considered him punished by God, stricken by him, and afflicted. **Matthew 4:24** News about him spread all over Syria, and people brought to him all who were ill with various diseases, those suffering severe pain, the demon-possessed, those having seizures, and the paralyzed; and he healed them.

DAILY DECLARATION

PRAYER:

Dear Lord, I give praise and glory today. I adore you and worship you. You are the almighty, ever living, and all powerful God. Thank you for always being there and for loving me unconditionally just the way I am!

Declare:

I am forgiven, I am well loved and highly favored. I may not feel like I am, but the truth is, I am the child of the most high God. He loves me in good times and in bad, in sickness and in health and forever and ever. My past has been washed away, and I am completely new because I am yours and you make me brand new. I surrender myself to you Lord. I believe you love me and care about me. I trust you; I trust you with my health, my life, my children, my future. I am your child. I am accepted and adopted into the family of God. I am a daughter/son of the most High God because of Jesus Christ who is my Lord and my God. Thank you, Lord, for sending Jesus to earth for me, to carry my sins and free me from all evil.

I am free from blemish, cleansed, holy and blameless in your sight because I am in Christ, and Christ chose me. I have been saved from God's wrath because I am in Christ, hidden in Him. I have been redeemed. I am your chosen possession. I choose to receive your love. I choose to believe you love me and accept me just the way I am. I receive your gift of freedom and life. I trust you, Lord.

TO REMIND YOU WHO YOU BELONG TO

PRAYER:

Thank you, Lord God for loving me and inviting me into your kingdom. No matter what I have done in the past, my sins are forgiven, and you welcome me with open arms and tell me I belong. I am your child. Thank you, heavenly Father.

DECLARE:

Jesus died for me. Jesus loves me.
God sent His son for me. Jesus sits at the right hand of the father forever interceding for me. Jesus became sin so I could become righteous.
I choose you Lord as Lord of my life and accept your forgiveness. I receive your forgiveness and declare that I am the righteousness of God in Christ Jesus. I am blessed because my sins are not only forgiven, but God Himself chose to forget them. The Lord protects me from all my enemies. No harm or disease, pestilence or disaster will come near me. My enemies will come at me from one direction but flee from me in seven. Thank you, Lord, for choosing me. I am your child.

GOD IS MY PROVIDER

PRAYER:

Father, I ask for help to trust you will provide for my family and me. Help me not to doubt. I want to be generous and free from worry regarding my future. I trust you, and your word which promises me provision, care, and all my needs met.

DECLARE:

The Lord will bless my family and me. He is my provider. I do not worry about anything. I trust God and will not fear or worry about my life, my future or my retirement. My eyes are on you. I am following you and seeking you. You are my shepherd, and I shall not want. You promise to shelter and feed me and take care of me. I am your child, and I will not go hungry. Those who seek the Lord will lack nothing (**Psalm 34:11**). That is your promise.

THEREFORE I DECLARE My barns are full and my vats are overflowing. Thank you, Lord, for restoring to me what the enemy has devoured. Thank you for returning to me what I have lost or thrown away and made a mess of. Thank you for rescuing me and my finances. Thank you, Lord, that my investments are restored and fattened and overflowing. Thank you that I am blessed and am a blessing and that all may know my God is the Lord, and that he takes care of all my needs according to his glorious riches.

Proverbs 3:9-10 "Honor the Lord with your wealth, with first fruits of all your produce; 10 Then will your barns be filled with plenty, with new wine your vats will overflow."

Philippians 4:19 "My God will fully supply whatever you need, in accord with his glorious riches in Christ Jesus."

Psalm 34:11 "The rich grow poor and go hungry, but those who seek the Lord lack no good thing."

Isaiah 49:23 " those who hope in the Lord will not be disappointed."

FOR THOSE ANXIOUS AND AFRAID

PRAYER:

Father, I ask for freedom from anxiety and fear. Lord take away these fearful thoughts, this nervous feeling. I need you Lord and trust that you are with me now at this very moment.

REFLECTION:

God says to us who will hear.... "Do not fear: I am with you; do not be anxious: I am your God. I will strengthen you, I will help you, I will uphold you with my victorious right hand" **(Is 41:10)**. What a promise! Who is that promise for? Anyone willing to hear it and believe it. ANYONE. Praise God.

DECLARE:

I am victorious. I am an overcomer. I am your child, your heir. I can do all things through you Jesus who strengthens me. I am strong in your mighty power, for your power is in me. When I am weak and afraid, you build me up. You Lord are my savior. You go before me and conquer my enemies, those who are too strong for me. I am at rest in you. My mind is at peace because my mind rests on you and your word. I believe you, Lord, when you say in your word that no weapon fashioned against me will prosper or harm me. I believe your word that says no harm will befall me and no disaster will come near my tent. My mind is yours, Lord. I command all my thoughts into obedience to You Lord Jesus. You are Lord of me and my thoughts. I am forgiven and free from all the past and all memories. You are my rock, the firm foundation on which I stand. I take refuge in you and I declare I am victorious. I am alive. I am healed. I am strong. I am more than a conqueror. I am perfectly and wonderfully made. I am your child. I am yours.

THOSE SEEKING FORGIVENESS

REFLECTION:

It is not our sins that keep us from God; it's our unwillingness to come to him for forgiveness. There is no condemnation for us who are in Christ Jesus. We are no longer condemned. Condemnation is for those who reject God's kingdom and choose to remain in darkness. I choose You Lord and Your kingdom. You are the way, the truth, and the life. In him, we are forgiven.

PRAYER:

Dear Father, I know I have done wrong in my heart and my actions. I have offended you. Please forgive me.

DECLARE:

I am forgiven. I turn away from all thoughts of unworthiness. I believe I am forgiven and cleansed from all unrighteousness. I thank you for the grace you lavish on me.

"If we confess our sins, He is faithful and righteous to forgive us our sins and to cleanse us from all unrighteousness," **(1 John 1:9).**

In him we have redemption by his blood, the forgiveness of transgressions, in accord with the riches of his grace [8] *that he lavished upon us* **(Ephesisans 1:7-8).**

PRAYER TO RECEIVE THE HOLY SPIRIT

PRAYER:

Fill us Lord with the Holy Spirit we declare our need for the Holy Spirit. We want to walk in the ways of the Spirit, not the flesh. We want to be controlled by the spirit, not our flesh. We choose you, Lord Jesus. We choose to receive the power of the Holy Spirit so that we can live for you and Our Lord. Holy Spirit enter my life so I may have....

POWER to know and love Christ

POWER to know the word of God

POWER to witness

POWER to act

POWER to live

POWER to represent God

POWER to show God's power through the gifts of the Holy Spirit

POWER to crush evil spirits

POWER to know God's will

POWER to remain in God's will

POWER to believe

POWER to proclaim the good news

DECLARE:

I am filled with the Holy Spirit. I have the power of the Holy Spirit in me. I walk, think and breathe with God's life in me. I am kind; I am joyful.
I have the joy of the Lord as my strength.
I am filled with peace and stay in peace.
I am self-controlled, gentle.
I am patient; I live in the Spirit, and my mind is on spiritual things.
I am not conceited, easily angered, envious or easily offended.
I do not throw fits of rage,
I am calm, full of wisdom and understanding.
I am thoughtful, considerate and compassionate.
I am not jealous or envious of others,
I am not self-centered or rude.
I am meek and humble not proud and boastful.
I do not spend time thinking evil thoughts.
I keep no record of others' faults and failings.
I do not delight in evil.
I am faithful and true.
I am trustworthy and honest.
I will love you, Lord, forever.
I can move mountains. I will not be shaken. I will not shrink back in the face of persecution. I will not fear though the earth give way and the mountains fall into the sea, though the waters roar and foam and the mountains quake. Even then will I be confident, because my confidence comes from you?

FIGHTING CANCER WITH SCRIPTURE

PRAYER:
Please, dear Lord, come to my aid and cleanse my body of all cancer.

DECLARE:
God anointed Jesus of Nazareth with the Holy Spirit and with power, and he went about doing good and healing all who were oppressed by the devil, for God was with Him (**Acts 10:38**), and he is still healing today. Cancer you are a defeated foe because the blood of Jesus was shed for me and he took all my sins and sickness with him on the cross for me (**Hebrews 2:14**).

I resist and know that cancer is fleeing from me because you Lord scatter my enemies and cause them to be defeated (**Deuteronomy 28:7**). Cancer is the enemy, and it is under my feet. I have the authority to trample on it, and it will not harm me (**Luke 10:19**). Thank you, Lord, for hearing my prayer, and I stand firm on your promise that I will live and not die but proclaim the works of the Lord (**Psalm 118:17**). To You, Lord Jesus be all the glory, honor and praise. May you be glorified in my healing and I declare this will not be passed down to my children or my grandchildren. I am taking a stand against its attack against me, and I will see the victory because my God is fighting for me (**Exodus 14:13-14**). God is with me, and I will not fear or be distressed. My faith in my God is firm and unwavering. He will come to my rescue and save me. My Lord is my rock, my strength, my fortress and my deliverer. He is my God in whom I trust, my rock of refuge, my shield, and my stronghold (**Psalm 18:3**). I believe God has better, more wonderful plans for me than suffering from cancer. I believe God has a future full of hope for me, not despair (**Jer 29:11**)

PRAYER TO REMAIN FREE

REFLECTION:
David didn't kill Goliath only to have him raise from the dead. He was killed. Permanently killed. He never reared his ugly head. If he had, David would have reminded him he was dead. David definitely would not listen to voices from the dead. He didn't pay attention to Goliath's words when he was alive. It's dead. If you still have fears of cancer returning, or depression or suicidal thoughts, it's time to put them to sleep forever. When God kills, it's permanent. Goliath didn't just die a physical death he died an eternal death. It's time to kill what is haunting you and permanently put it to rest. Remember who healed you. Remind yourself that you are healed and the disease is gone. The Bible says "Submit yourselves to God. Resist the devil, and he will flee from you. Draw near to God, and he will draw near to you"(James 4:7-8).

DECLARE:
This devil was beaten!!! _____ has no hold on me and has fled at your rebuke. _____ was defeated, killed, destroyed and buried. God, I know you healed me, and you are never allowing this evil to come near me again. You are my rock, my fortress, and my savior. You are my protection, my shield, the power that saved me. You Lord Jesus are my hiding place and my rock of refuge. No harm can come near me. You saved me from my enemies "By his stripes, I am healed" I am healed. I believe Jesus healed me and I will not entertain thoughts that tell me differently. God is with me. The Greater One lives in me, and I will have length of days. I will be healthy and live an abundant, full and fruitful life. None of the diseases of the Egyptians are on us his children; we are set apart, and cancer is far from us. Hallelujah! The blessing of God is mine today and forever because I belong to Christ. Healing is my gift from God, and it is irrevocable. Our Savior lives, he died and was buried, and by the same spirit that lives in us he was raised from the

dead and now, because of his great love for us, sits at the right hand of power forever interceding for us. Jesus is our lord and savior, and we are his great reward.

Hebrews 2:14 *Now since the children share in blood and flesh, he likewise shared in them, that through death he might destroy the one who has the power of death, that is, the devil,*

James 4:7 *Submit yourselves, then, to God. Resist the devil, and he will **flee** from you.*

Acts 10:38 *God anointed Jesus of Nazareth with the Holy Spirit and with power, who went about doing good and healing all who were oppressed by the devil, for God was with Him.*

Psalm 44:5 *Through You we will push back our adversaries; Through Your name we will trample down those who rise up against us.*

Luke 10:19 *"Behold, I have given you authority to tread on serpents and scorpions, and over all the power of the enemy, and nothing will injure you.*

Deuteronomy 28:7 *"The Lord will beat down before you the enemies that rise up against you; they will come out against you from one direction, and flee before you in seven.*

Luke 10:19 *Behold, I give you the authority to trample on serpents and scorpions, and over all the power of the enemy, and nothing shall by any means hurt you.*

Psalm 118:17 *I shall not die, but live, And declare the works of the Lord.*

Matthew 8:17 *"He Himself took our infirmities And bore our sicknesses."*

Exodus 14:13-14 *"Do not fear! Stand your ground and see the victory the Lord will win for you today. For these Egyptians whom you see today you will never see again. ¹⁴ The Lord will fight for you; you have only to keep still."*

2 Chronicles 20:17 *You will not have to fight in this encounter. Take your places, stand firm, and see the salvation of the Lord; he will be with you, Judah and Jerusalem. Do not fear or be dismayed. Tomorrow go out to meet them, and the Lord will be with you."*

Psalm 34:4 *This poor man cried out, and the Lord heard him, and saved him out of all his troubles.*

Psalm 18:3 *Lord, my rock, my fortress, my deliverer, My God, my rock of refuge, my shield, my saving horn, my stronghold!*

Psalm 41:4 *The Lord sustains him on his sickbed*

Deut 20:4 *For it is the Lord, your God, who goes with you to fight for you against your enemies and give you victory."*

Jeremiah 29:11 *'For I know the plans that I have for you,'declares the LORD, 'plans for welfare and not for calamity to give you a future and a hope.*

BECAUSE OF JESUS YOU CAN DECLARE:

I am the righteousness of God in Christ Jesus (2 Corinthians 5:21)
I am healed (Isaiah 53:5)
I am favored (Psalm 5:12)
I am a joint heir with Jesus (Romans 8:17)
Everything I put my hand to will prosper (3 John 1:2)
I am accepted and approved (Ephesians 1:6)
I will have a long life (Psalm 91:16)

Thoughts follow our words, faith follows our words: So let's speak in faith though we may not yet believe it or see it. Let's say it anyway.

I am a good provider.
I am a good wife, mother.
I am a good Father, husband.
I am healthy. I am trustworthy. I am bold.
I am confident. I walk by faith not by sight.
I am well, I am healed.
My God supplies all of my needs.

PRAYER FOR THOSE ON CHEMO

Mark 16:17-18 *These signs will accompany those who believe............ 18 They will pick up serpents [with their hands], and if they drink any deadly thing, it will not harm them.....*

PRAYER:

Jesus said that we (as believers) will drink deadly poison and it will not harm us.

Father, many of us, are on medicine and taking chemo treatments. We as one body of Christ are asking and trusting in your protection as they receive treatment. We are trusting your word which says that when we, your children, drink deadly poison, it will not hurt us. We praise your Holy Name and thank you, Father, that all the medicines we take are only doing what they are supposed to and nothing else. We trust you, God. Thank you, God, that cancer is leaving our bodies in the name of Jesus.

WHEN IN THE BATTLE

PRAYER:

Father carry _____ when they get tired of believing and praising and want to give up.

DECLARE:

Declaring for _____ especially today our sisters who are in the battle... The lord is our strength, our rock, our fortress, our deliverer, our God, our rock of refuge. He is a Shield, our saving horn, and our stronghold. Cancer is Goliath, and he is dead. Anxiety is Goliath, and he is dead and not coming back to life. God didn't raise up Goliath, and he is not resurrecting this demon coming against you. Goliath did not rise from the dead and follow David around speaking to him and taunting him. No David killed Goliath. YOU HAVE TO KILL. You are victorious and more than a conqueror. The battle rages but the war is won, and we declare our confidence in our God who saves, our God who heals

I put no confidence in my ability to save myself. I am hopeless without you Lord, but with you, I can move mountains, I can raise dead bones to life, and I can lay hands on the sick, and they will get well. I can do all things through Christ who strengthens me.

Philippians 4:13 I have the strength for everything through him who empowers me.

Psalm 27 Though an army besiege me, though war break out against me I will remain confident in you oh lord.

Deuteronomy 31:6 "Be strong and courageous, do not be afraid or tremble at them, for the LORD your God is the one who goes with you He will not fail you or forsake you."

Psalm 18:39 For You have girded me with strength for battle; You have subdued under me those who rose up against me.

Deuteronomy 20:1 "When you go out to battle against your enemies and see horses and chariots and people more numerous than you, do not be afraid of them; for the LORD your God, who brought you up from the land of Egypt, is with you.

Isaiah 41:1 'Do not fear, for I am with you; Do not anxiously look about you, for I am your God I will strengthen you, surely I will help you, Surely I will uphold you with My righteous right hand.'

Psalm 138:7 Though I walk in the midst of trouble, You will revive me; You will stretch forth Your hand against the wrath of my enemies, And Your right hand will save me.

PRAYER FOR YOUR MIND

PRAYER:

Lord, my mind is so scattered and fragmented today. My thoughts spin, spiral and get out of control. Help me to have clear thoughts and a productive mind.

DECLARE:

You have the mind of Christ so look out world. My mind is perfect and in perfect peace when it remains on him and in his word. Jesus loves me; I am a child of the King of all Kings. I choose Jesus, and I am perfectly and wonderfully made. I have the mind of Christ because the Bible says so. The bible says because I believe in Jesus and trust him; I am his and all that belongs to him is mine. The bible says I have the mind of Christ, so I reject all negative thoughts. I command my thoughts into the obedience to Christ Jesus my Lord and God. Thank you, Lord, for healing me and giving me abundant, healthy life.

For, although we are in the flesh, we do not battle according to the flesh, for the weapons of our battle are not of flesh but are enormously powerful, capable of destroying fortresses. We destroy arguments , and every pretension raising itself against the knowledge of God, and take every thought captive in obedience to Christ **2 Cor 10:3**

For "who has known the mind of the Lord, so as to counsel him?" But we have the mind of Christ." (1 Corinthians 2:16)

DEMENTIA

PRAYER:

Lord, I fear the thought of Dementia. I am afraid it will take hold of me. I am afraid it will be passed down to my children. Protect me from this illness. My trust is in You. Help me and come to rescue.

DECLARE:

I am free from dementia, and even the threat of it is gone in the name of Jesus. Jesus is Lord, and I have the mind of Christ. I have been born again and has no history of any disease looming over me or mine. We rebuke the demonic powers that threaten us and command them to leave. The blood of Jesus covers me and is delivering me from all fear. I am walking in victory and am victorious for my sake and the sake of my family. I am passing on a new legacy. One of health, vigor and faith and trust. The devil hates me because I am standing in faith and will not be moved.

We need to stand and fight with our family members every day and declare this over those afflicted and suffering or fearful every day.

REPEAT - I am more than a conqueror through my father and myLord Jesus. Lord you are my protection, and I thank you for commanding your angels to protect me from all harm and from the spiritual forces of evil coming against me. We put on the armor of God to protect us, and we lift up the shield of faith. Jesus is Lord of my body.

WHAT TO SAY WHEN DEPRESSED:

DECLARE:

"I belong to Jesus.
I am his daughter, and you are trespassing on private property.
I was bought and paid for.
SAY IT EVERYDAY TILL YOU BELIEVE IT!!!
DEVIL, YOU ARE A LIAR!
Today is a great day.
Jesus is Lord of my life.
The Blood of Jesus has rescued me from power of darkness
These feelings are lies.
This depression is a lie.
I am well; I am whole because Jesus made me whole.
The Lord forgives all my sins and heals all my diseases.
He redeems me from the pit and crowns me with love and compassion.
I am healed because he bore my sickness and disease. He bore my pain.
By his stripes, I am healed.
God has delivered me from every evil.
I have been redeemed from the curse.
My God has delivered me from the power of darkness and conveyed *me* into the kingdom of the Son of His love.
I am filled to overflowing with the Holy Spirit.
The Holy Spirit lives in me, and GREATER IS HE THAT IS IN ME THAN YOU DEVIL.
I command my mind to obey JESUS CHRIST.
I take authority over my mind and command it to obey you, Lord Jesus. I command all my thoughts into submission.
I lift up the shield of faith as protection from every voice and word that is not of God.
You are LORD of my mind."

WHEN THOUGHTS, MEMORIES OR NIGHTMARES COME....

When wicked thoughts come and you don't have control.....
When dreams or nightmares come....
When you can't get images or memories out of your head
Put your hands on your head and say......

I have the mind of Christ.	1 Cor 2:16
I choose to set my mind on things above.	Col 3:2
Renew my mind Lord.	Rom 12:1-2
I take every thought captive and make Them obedient to Christ.	2 Cor 10:6

This is my mind and I take authority over it
And cast out all imaginations or wicked thoughts.
You Lord Jesus are Lord of my thoughts and dreams, I trust you.

Philippians 4:8-9 *Finally, brothers, whatever is true, whatever is noble,*
whatever is right, whatever is pure, whatever is lovely,
whatever is admirable—if anything is excellent or praiseworthy—
think about such things. Whatever you have learned or received
or heard from me, or seen in me—put it into practice.
And the God of peace will be with you

About the Author

Marybeth has been in ministry to Catholic Community for over 30 years. She began as a CCD Teacher at St. Bartholomew Catholic Church in Katy Texas where she served for ten years as a teacher and prayer group leader. Marybeth was a core team leader of the Spirit-Filled Prayer Group and co-led Life in the Spirit Seminars during that time.

Marybeth and her husband Mark moved to McKinney, Texas in 1999 with their three children, Faith, Peter, and David where they joined The St. Gabriel Catholic Community. Marybeth attended CRHP in 2004 and became Spiritual Director of CRHP 2. She began a Women's Bible Study immediately afterward with a few CRHP sisters, and it is still thriving to this day with well over 100 participants each year. Marybeth leads the weekly Women's Bible Study as well as a weekly prayer group meeting, gives lectures, leads annual retreats and is a writer and speaker.

Other publications:

Taking Control of Your Mind and Your Thoughts,
According to Your Faith - 15 Week Bible Study
Holy Spirit, The Lord and Giver of Life - 28 Week Bible Study
31 Days - A Devotional
A.C.T.S Prayer
Healing Scriptures - FREE DOWNLOAD
www.where2ormoregather.com/documents/healing-scriptures/

mbwuenschel@gmail.com
www.where2ormoregather.com
https://www.facebook.com/catholicdevotional/

Made in the USA
Charleston, SC
02 January 2017